# 7 Steps To Reconnect With Your Guardian Angel

## *A Divine Journey*

Marguerite Davies

4th Generation Celtic Healer
Angelic Spiritual Master Teacher

Foreword by Michelle Davies

Award-Winning Author

7 Steps to Reconnect with Your Guardian Angel: A Divine Journey



For permission requests or inquiries, please contact the author at:
Marguerite Davies
1 Lilac Cottage, Martley Road
Worcester, WR2 6QG
United Kingdom
Email: rita@healingtouch.uk.com

Disclaimer:
The content of this book is intended for informational and inspirational purposes only. The spiritual guidance, practices and individual experiences shared by the author are not meant to substitute for professional advice, whether legal, medical, psychological, or otherwise. Readers are encouraged to consult a qualified professional before undertaking any new spiritual, health-related, or legal actions based on the material provided in this book.

ISBN:978-1-0369-1543-8

Printed in the United Kingdom

Published by: Marguerite Davies

# Contents

# Heartfelt Blessing

*May your Guardian Angel walk beside you,*
*guiding, comforting and lighting your path.*
*May you feel their love in every moment,*
*their wisdom in every choice,*
*their peace in every breath.*

*May your days be abundant with love,*
*your heart full of joy, your life overflowing with health and prosperity.*
*May you find kindness in unexpected places.*
*And light even in the darkest moments.*

*You are never alone.*
*You are held, cherished and deeply loved.*
*This is a blessing from my heart to all of humanity*
*from one beating heart to another.*

With love light and blessings,
***Marguerite***

# Acknowledgements

I would like to express my deepest gratitude to my dear husband Gary, for your unwavering patience, understanding and steadfast belief in me. You have been my rock and your support has been a constant source of strength for which I am eternally grateful.

To my children and precious grandchildren, as well as those awaiting in spirit, you are my anchors, my inspiration and my greatest joy. Our shared adventures in the magical fairyland garden, sparks my imagination and fills my heart with joy and wonder.

To my siblings, nieces, nephews and cousins you have all have enriched my life with lessons, unconditional love and forgiveness. My heartfelt thanks extend especially to my family in spirit: my parents, grandparents, my sister Rosemary, a remarkable scholar, your influence has been a profound reminder of divine love, kindness and the importance of self-love, my brother Moss and aunts, uncles, in-laws and friends.

Your presence is as close now as ever and I feel your guidance daily during meditation.

I am deeply grateful to my dear kindred spirits Jacqui, Linda, Amba, Michelle, Kate Lin, Auriol and the many acquaintances who have brightened my journey. Special thanks go to my son Matt and niece, Michelle whose support, encouragement and insights were invaluable throughout this writing process.

To my incredible clients, I am profoundly honoured by the trust you have placed in me during your healing journeys. It has been a privilege to support you in reconnecting with your true source of love. I also extend my gratitude to the authors whose works have profoundly influenced my journey.

Your wisdom has illuminated my path, enriched my understanding of spirituality and deepened my connection to the mind, body and spirit:

Robert James Comber, The Lost Octave: Our Story in the Stars

Alice A. Bailey, Esoteric Psychology, Vol. 1: A Treatise on the Seven Rays

Drunvalo Melchizedek, The Ancient Secret of the Flower of Life, Volumes 1 & 2

Soozi Holbeche, The Power of Gems and Crystals: How They Can Transform Your Life

Thich Nhat Hanh, The Miracle of Mindfulness: The Classic Guide

Dr. Joshua David Stone, The Golden Book of Melchizedek, Volume 2: How to Become an Integrated Christ/Buddha in this Lifetime, Soul Psychology Keys to Ascension.

H.P. Blavatsky, The Land of the Gods: The Long-Hidden Story of Visiting the Masters of Wisdom in Shambhala

Alan Hopking, Esoteric Healing: A Practical Guide Based on the Teachings of the Tibetan in the Works of Alice A. Bailey.

Finally, I give heartfelt thanks to the Divine Creator, God, Goddess whose love and light continue to guide my life and work.

With love and blessings from Marguerite

# Introduction

Have you ever felt a presence guiding you through intuition, signs and synchronicities? A yearning, an inner knowing that there is more to life, more than what we can see, touch, or explain? What if the ancient wisdom of healers, the lost knowledge of Atlantis and the power of divine connection were waiting for you to rediscover?

*7 Steps to Reconnecting with Your Guardian Angel – A Divine Journey* is more than just a guide. It is an invitation to awaken your spiritual gifts, deepen your connection to the angelic realm and align your life with divine purpose. Infused with peace, love and ancient wisdom, this book offers practical tools and divinely inspired insights to help you strengthen your connection with your Guardian Angel and unlock your highest potential.

This book holds the secrets to embracing every dream and wish available to you.

Written by Marguerite, a fourth-generation Celtic healer, Master Angelic Teacher and holistic practitioner, this book unveils long-lost spiritual teachings, bridging ancient traditions with modern revelations. Guided by the wisdom of her Guardian Angel, Mena, Marguerite shares profound insights and practical techniques to help you reconnect with divine guidance and step into your highest self.

These divine transmissions form the foundation for humanity's awakening to its true destiny of ascension. They arrive at a time when we are being called to rise, to heal and to return to love.

Whether you are just beginning your self -healing spiritual journey or an experienced practitioner or teacher, this guide echoes timeless angelic teachings woven with healing techniques rooted in the lost wisdom of Atlantis. Each chapter adds new layers of ancient knowledge while introducing powerful tools for aligning with divine energy and accessing intuitive guidance including crystal grids, sacred geometry, numerology (with angelic numbers), pendulum dowsing and unique channelled meditations.

This book was not created in the traditional sense it was received through divine communion, quiet reflection and inner prompting. Mena's voice became clear, guiding Marguerite to bring forward teachings hidden for lifetimes. These steps are not only about individual healing; they are part of a collective awakening, a remembrance of who we truly are at the soul level.

We are living in a time of powerful energetic shift. The balance of the Divine Feminine and Divine Masculine is being restored within each of us and across the planet. This sacred union awakens our wholeness. When we stand in Divine Spirit rooted in love and light we embody empowered kindness, compassion, clarity, strength and wisdom. We open to the radiance of the Divine God and the Divine Goddess within and through this harmony, we align with the universal flow of creation.

In this journey, you will explore channelled meditations from higher realms, including transmissions believed to originate from Atlantean priestesses and Archangels. You'll discover true stories of healing and transformation from individuals who have reawakened their angelic connection, as well as angelic tools and techniques to support your own healing practice and spiritual path.

Through this journey, you will learn to:

- Reconnect with your Guardian Angel and strengthen your divine bond
- Harness angelic self-healing practices to restore balance to yourself, loved ones, pets, animals, Earth the Universe

- Access the sacred teachings of Atlantis, awakening the inner knowledge of high priests and priestesses
- Raise your vibration and manifest peace, joy and harmony in your daily life
- Deepen your intuitive bond and spiritual awareness through guided meditations, visualisations and ancient healing practices.

Each page of this book carries intentional energy. It is infused with the frequency of divine remembrance, love and empowerment.

You may notice subtle shifts within you as you read or receive insights that feel divinely inspired. This is the Divine presence guiding you walking beside you in light.

You may choose to move through the 7 Steps in sequence, allowing the energy to build naturally, or trust your intuition and begin where you're called. Before reading, you are encouraged to create a quiet space, light a candle, breathe deeply and call upon your Guardian Angel. This book is not only a guide it is a living companion for your soul's development.

Every chapter also holds true events real and moving moments when Mena, Marguerite's Guardian Angel, appeared in times of need.

These stories are gently woven throughout, offering reassurance and inspiration and revealing how divine presence flows into our lives in the most unexpected and grace-filled ways.

Among the most profound of these moments are those shared with her children. Mena's spirit often came forward through their words, their dreams and their intuitive hearts, offering guidance, comfort and deep understanding. These chapters illustrate how being both neurodivergent and empathic is not only manageable but deeply meaningful when embraced with love and support.

Marguerite offers this guidance with the hope of bringing light to parents and especially of neurodivergent children, reminding them that their children are not broken they are beautifully attuned. They are radiant, emotionally intelligent souls who are here with purpose.

With the right support and spiritual re-connection, their sensitivity can become their strength and their inner world can shine in ways the world is just beginning to understand.

My heartfelt wish is that through these 7 Steps, you begin to feel this connection more deeply to trust in the wisdom that flows through you and to embrace the love that has always been your birthright.

It is my belief The 7 Steps to Reconnect with Your Guardian Angel is more than a spiritual practice. It is the foundation for humanity's ascension a bridge between the seen and unseen, a pathway to awakening. This is an invitation to step into your highest self and live with clarity, joy, love and divine purpose by:

1. Preparing a sacred space for angelic healing, creating an environment of peace and high vibration
2. Creating a sacred altar, anchoring your connection with the angelic realm
3. Grounding and balancing your energy centres, strengthening your energetic foundation
4. Reconnecting with your Guardian Angel, opening the channel for divine communication
5. Awakening the divine potential within, embracing your higher intelligence and limitless capabilities
6. Closing your sacred space and grounding excess energy, sealing your spiritual work with balance
7. Gratitude grounding, cultivating an open heart to receive divine blessings

These steps are not simply about personal transformation they are part of a greater awakening. The wisdom of the ancients, the sacred knowledge of Atlantis and the divine intelligence that has guided souls for millennia are rising to the surface now, at the perfect moment for our collective evolution.

I share these teachings with deep love and a genuine desire to support you on this path. Everyone can develop their higher intelligence, deepen their intuition and step into their divine potential.

This is not reserved for a select few it is a divine birthright available to all.

As you continue forward, know that you are guided, supported and deeply loved. Over time, you may find that asking for divine guidance becomes as natural as breathing.

What once felt like a practice becomes a way of being a quiet, steady presence in your life, gently leading you towards greater peace, wisdom and joy.

Let the light of the angelic realm and the ancient energy of Atlantis support your return to wholeness. May you walk forward in balance, embracing both the Divine God and the Divine Goddess within you.

Your Guardian Angel is gently calling

Are you ready to listen?

***Marguerite***

# Praise for the Author

I am deeply humbled and grateful for the opportunity to share my gifts and to walk alongside so many on their journeys of healing and spiritual growth. Each person we meet enlightens our soul in some way, even the people we don't like, reminding us that nothing is a coincidence.

Life often surprises us with new lessons, new opportunities for growth and new ways to connect with the God and Goddess within.

These testimonials come from individuals whose paths I have had the honour of crossing. Their words reflect not just their journeys, but also the beauty of what we can achieve when we embrace our own light and step into our highest potential. May their stories inspire you to reconnect with the love, guidance and infinite possibilities that surround you."

*"Rita's healing circles are sacred spaces where profound transformation occurs. Her clairvoyance and connection to spirit guide us effortlessly into realms of intuition and wisdom. Every experience with her leaves me energised, inspired and ready to step forward in life with clarity."*

AMBA GATHERUM-MATTHEWS,
YOGA GURU

*"Rita's therapies not only healed my body but uplifted my soul. Her devotion to the healing arts is unparalleled and her presence is a gift to all who encounter her."*

LINDA MORGAN, MSC,
REGISTERED PSYCHOTHERAPIST AND TRAUMA SPECIALIST

*"Rita has without a doubt changed my life. The word that comes to mind when I think of her is support. When I first met Rita, I was already on a spiritual path and in some ways, thought I knew it all. But Rita helped me realise how ungrounded I was. She gently guided me to ground my spiritual knowledge, always offering unconditional support and making me feel valued and understood in a world where I often felt disconnected. Her Angelic Reiki training and monthly meditations were invaluable, preparing me and many others, to navigate the profound changes unfolding in the world.*

*Rita is a true pioneer who was working in the healing field long before it became mainstream. She has helped me through some of the most challenging times of my life and I have always felt deeply supported by her love."*

AURIOL BURGESS,
HOLISTIC LIFE COACH AND HEALER

*"Rita's depth of knowledge and emotional support are tremendous. I felt happy, safe and secure in her presence. She taught me so much more than I expected, confirming my own thoughts and feelings and helping me trust in the Angels and Ascended Masters."*

MICHELLE C.,
SPIRITUAL HEALER AND HOLISTIC THERAPIST

*"Rita has walked alongside me during some of the darkest and most challenging periods of my life. For that I am eternally grateful.*

*In the early years, when my appointments were to get me through another punishing month at work, I was completely unaware of the silent healing Rita also gave me each time we met.*

*As health conditions slowly emerged and which I now realise were also "spirit" messages that it was time to look at my life, Rita was there to gently guide, heal and prepare me for the time when I would be called upon to help heal myself.*

*That time arrived when I was diagnosed with cancer and it was not met with fear. Instead, absolute trust and peace of mind that all would be well and an intense period of inner healing and faith with Rita at my side.*

*I acknowledged that the medical procedure was necessary to remove parts that were no longer of any service to my body and am grateful to the excellent care I received from the surgeons and nurses.*

*To have faith and trust in God and know that you have the ability, should you choose; to help heal yourself is the most wonderful gift any human being can give to another. Thank you, Rita."*

JACQUI BAYLISS
TRUSTEE

*"Rita's story is a testament to the beauty of being human, a life lived with open arms and an open heart. She constantly shares her light with the world and beyond. Rita is a radiant example of what it means to grow in spirit, love deeply and inspire others to do the same."*

ANDREA BSc,
MENTAL HEALTH FACILITATOR

*"To all those who have shared their journeys with me, I extend my heartfelt gratitude. Each story reminds me of the boundless potential within us all and the light that connects us. As you read this book and embrace your own spiritual path, I encourage you to let your light shine brightly. We are all beacons, here to guide one another and to illuminate the way toward love, healing and transformation. Together, we create ripples of light that can inspire the world.*

*Thank you for allowing me to share this journey with you."*

MARGUERITE DAVIES
AUTHOR

# Foreword

When my Aunt, Rita Davies, invited me to write the foreword for *7 Steps to Reconnecting with Your Guardian Angel – A Divine Journey*, I was deeply honoured. Our connection goes beyond family; it is a sacred bond rooted in our shared path as healers. Over the years, we have supported and inspired each other, exchanging healing modalities and witnessing the profound transformation that comes from divine alignment.

What makes this book truly extraordinary is that it reflects not only Rita's immense wisdom but also the echoes of our ancestral lineage. Our family's history, steeped in the healing traditions of Ireland, flows through the pages of this work. Rita's words are imbued with the love and sacred energy of those who came before us, making this book a deeply personal offering to the world.

*7 Steps to Reconnecting with Your Guardian Angel* is much more than a guide; it is a divine invitation. Rita reminds us that spiritual connection is not reserved for the few but is an innate gift we can all reclaim. Whether you are new to this journey or a seasoned seeker, these seven steps will meet you exactly where you are, offering practical tools, meditations and affirmations to help you embrace your highest potential.

As someone who has dedicated my life to empowering others to heal and grow, I can say with certainty that this book has the power to transform lives. Rita's guidance is not just about personal growth, it is about reconnecting with the light within you and radiating that light outward, touching the lives of others and contributing to the ascension of humanity.

May this book inspire you to trust in the divine presence that surrounds you always. May it remind you that your Guardian Angel walks beside you, offering love and guidance as you rediscover your soul's purpose. As you turn each page, may you feel a sense of profound connection, to your Guardian Angel, your ancestors and the universal energy that unites us all. With love and blessings

***Michelle Davies***
Award-Winning Author.

CHAPTER 1

# The 7 Steps to Reconnect with Your Guardian Angel

## *My Early Journey*

Every journey begins with a quiet calling, an inner knowing from within that beckons us to see the world from a unique perspective. For me that calling emerged early, as a deep sensitivity to the unseen forces of nature. Though often isolating, this sensitivity opened a gateway to a profound spiritual connection that transformed my understanding of existence.

In the following pages, I share the tender beginnings of my spiritual journey, a path illuminated by a sacred inheritance of healing, a profound connection to the natural world and the loving presence of my Guardian Angel Mena. Always by my side Mena offers unwavering support with gentle compassion and kindness. She does not push or impose but lovingly allows me the freedom to discover my own way, free from judgment or discipline. As a divine messenger she agreed to guide me through this life, a sacred promise made before my incarnation. Her presence continually reminds me that I am enveloped by a force of nurturing unconditional love.

Although angels are without gender, I have always resonated with the vision of Mena as a female form, inspired by the lovely bond I share with my mother and my three sisters, four extraordinary souls who have shaped my understanding of love and connection.

## *Embracing Solitude: A Journey of Divine Connection and Spiritual Awakening*

From an early age I sensed a spiritual sensitivity within me an innate gift that set me apart, though I did not fully grasp its significance at the time. My mother however recognised it clearly. She nurtured this heightened awareness, noticing my deep connection to the life force flowing through all living things.

This connection extended far beyond my refusal to eat meat or fish; it was an understanding that all creatures great and small carried the same divine energy that pulsed within me. I felt their presence their essence, as though bound by an invisible thread of love that united every living being.

## *Finding My Place Beyond the Norm*

This sacred sensitivity is a spiritual inheritance passed down through generations of our family. Children and animals were drawn to me, instinctively trusting the light and love within me. I did not merely observe the world around me; I was attuned to it. Though beautiful this gift often left me feeling different and isolated. Even in solitude I sensed this gift was shaping my soul's understanding of love, empathy and the divine presence that quietly guides us all.

At one point, my sister studying to become a teacher chose to make me the subject of a case study. She noted that I seemed withdrawn and unhappy, unaware of the profound inner world I was experiencing. To help me connect with others she suggested I transfer to a local school, hoping a change of environment might allow me to find friends and a sense of belonging. Though my mother agreed with hesitation, she sensed the complexity of my nature. This decision marked the beginning of a new phase, where I navigated a world foreign to my rich spiritual experiences.

Attending the new school thrust me into a realm of conventionality, where the formality of social life and school routines did not align with my spiritual awareness. The conversations and interactions felt disconnected from the deep connection I had with nature, animals and the divine energy that pulsed within and around me. I took part in daily activities but often felt like an outsider, observing rather than engaging. My connection to the natural world seemed misplaced in the structured environment of school, leaving me feeling even more isolated.

During this time of confusion and uncertainty Mena was ever-present. She would gently use words of wisdom, "All is well," a mantra that became my guiding light.

Her gentle reassurances were like a lifeline, reminding me that I was never truly alone, even when I felt disconnected from others. Her guidance was subtle, compassionate and full of patience. She was not there to direct my steps but to support me as I found my own path

## *The Sacred Legacy of Healing: A Family Gift of Divine Love*

Our family carries a profound legacy of healing a sacred gift known simply as *"the cure."* This divine ability has flowed through the generations, passed down like a cherished prayer from my Great, Great-Grandmother to my Grandmother, women of unwavering strength, deep compassion and unshakable faith. Throughout Southern Ireland, they were known not only for their gift of healing people but also for their tender care of animals. Their hands were instruments of unconditional love, a love that transcended suffering, hardship and time itself.

My mother would often recount stories from the dark days of the troubles, when famine and oppression weighed heavily upon our people. As Catholic farmers, our ancestors shared what little food they had with those in need, their generosity an unspoken act of defiance against cruelty. My Great-Grandmother, risking punishment under unjust laws, became a hedge teacher, secretly educating children in the hidden corners of the land. These women, guided by their sacred hearts, embodied the very essence of love, courage and service, even in the face of adversity.

As a child, my mother faced near-death experiences three times. Each time, my grandfather would race down the lane, her limp body in his arms, desperate to reach the local doctor. Through these harrowing trials, her life was miraculously saved. She often spoke of a young woman from her village who, with unwavering faith, prayed a nightly vigil for her recovery. That act of devotion, coupled with divine love, allowed my mother to survive and grow into a strong woman who would bear seven children a living testament to God's miracles.

Living proof of *"the cure,"* she experienced its power early in her marriage when she sprained her ankle. My father carried her to parents home sat her down and asked for the' cure'

His mother, a woman gifted with the sacred art of healing passed this cherished gift to her son, my uncle, a kind sincere man. He then used it to heal her injury by wrapping her ankle in lint placing holy water upon and saying a prayer. This was more than a family tradition; it was an act of unconditional love, a divine responsibility and a sacred blessing carefully carried forward through generations.

## *Calling Upon the Divine Feminine*

At the heart of our family's spiritual life is the Divine Feminine. As devout Catholics, we turn to Mother Mary, Queen of Angels, Mother of God, not only as a religious figure but as the embodiment of nurturing, compassion and divine strength. She is the sacred force that has flowed through our lineage for centuries, honoured in both ancient Celtic traditions and Catholic devotion. To us, she represents the harmony between woman, life, nature and spirit.

Through this sacred connection, we invoke her grace in times of healing, seeking her loving intercession to restore balance and well-being. Our prayers, though simple, carry the wisdom and weight of generations. When we call upon Mother Mary, we do not merely ask for help, we reach for the timeless thread that connects us to our ancestors, to the land and to the divine.

In her, we see the purest expression of unconditional love, a love that transcends suffering, bringing peace to the weary and light to the lost. Her intercession is the bridge between the earthly and the sacred, allowing the healer's hands to channel something far greater: a divine energy that soothes the body, mends the spirit and uplifts the soul.

This is the heart of our lineage. This is our sacred gift.

## *What is a Guardian Angel?*

From my personal experience a Guardian Angel is a true living being more than a celestial energy, it is a higher wisdom, intelligence and an inseparable part of your soul's divine journey. As your higher self your Guardian Angel embodies the purest and most complete version of who you are created with a sacred purpose to, guide and protect your soul on its path through both earthly and spiritual realms.

Unlike humans a Guardian Angel is genderless and without physical form, existing solely as a profound and radiant presence of divine energy, embodying the highest frequencies of love, light and compassion. This energy is not constrained by the limits of the physical world, instead transcending multiple dimensions allowing your Guardian Angel to be fully with you wherever you go.

Guardian Angels are a manifestation of one's higher intelligence, with gentle unconditional loving presence as messengers of God, beings of pure radiant energy, here to support and uplift through every twist and turn of daily life.

I know these Angelic beings exist on such a high frequency, so beautifully subtle that we many do not perceive them with our physical eyes.

Yet we may hear a high octave of sound or an inner knowing in our hearts. In quiet moments of stillness when the mind is focussed you may have a gentle feeling of warmth, or an intuitive knowing reminding us of their presence assuring that we are never truly alone.

They connect with us through the language of light energy, a soft vibration that links us within a vast web of life love and consciousness. How could we not be open to the possibilities that awaits, when each of us holds the power to create a vision of peace and fulfilment within ourselves.

The essence of a Guardian Angel is compassion patience and unconditional love a reflection of the divine light that connects all souls. They are here to guide us not only through the trials of the physical world but through the profound spiritual journey that calls us to grow and transform aligning with the higher truths of our soul's path gently guiding us back to the light within.

Many may not sense their presence or think to give thanks to our Guardian Angels. However, they are always, waiting patiently for us to reconnect with our truest authentic selves. All we need to do is listen and the quiet song of our soul, will lead us back to the light they hold for us with unwavering love.

## *Remembering the Divine Symphony*

Mena, my Guardian Angel, shared with me a vision of the divine plan, a vision that has reshaped my understanding of purpose and connection. She described the Creator as a master composer, with each soul as a unique note in a grand ever-unfolding symphony of existence. Each of us has a sacred purpose, a promise to contribute something precious to the universe, something that helps it expand in love, beauty and wisdom. This purpose is a unique offering of the qualities that only you can bring. When we embrace this purpose, we are not merely living; we are harmonising with the eternal dance of creation itself, an orchestra of spirit that resonates across all time and space.

Mena revealed human beings often forget their divine purpose due to the busy materialistic world we live in. Full of distractions stress, challenges often pulled away from the love and harmony that are our soul's natural state. This may be due to negative forces rooted in fear separation and negativity creating discord both within and around us, steering us away from the harmony that exists within. These influences are not part of the Creator's vision nor of our soul's deepest desires. However, the melody of your soul, the music of our true self, is one of peace, joy, contentment and love. This truth is always present like a song waiting for you to remember and embrace.

The journey back to harmony is within the sacred heart reconnecting with your divine spirit and Guardian Angel.

## *Ascension - Aligning with Our True Nature*

As I share the beginning of my spiritual journey one marked by a sacred inheritance of healing, a profound connection to nature and the loving guidance of my Guardian Angel, Mena, I hope to illuminate your own path of loving - kindness. May this journey inspire awakening to inner knowing, your sixth sense, self-discovery and a gentle reconnection with the love and wisdom that have always resided within you. This path is rich with lessons in compassion, acceptance, trust, resilience and unconditional love.

It is gently inviting you to embark on your own journey, back to joy, harmony, peace, love of your true authentic self and the sacred guidance that patiently awaits you.[information in Chapter 6]

## *Guardian Angels and the Divine Journey*

Across cultures and spiritual traditions, it is believed that each of us carries both a soul and a spirit. The soul is our unique essence while the spirit is the infinite force that breathes life into all things and connects us to the greater whole.

In this beautiful interplay of unique individuality and unity human life becomes a sacred expression of Divine Creation.

This understanding is as ancient as humanity itself. The belief in Guardian Angels transcends time embedded into the spiritual heritage of countless traditions. These celestial companions walk beside us from birth and beyond offering protection guidance and unconditional love as we journey through life. As messengers of the Divine, they whisper gentle reminders of our connection to love wisdom and the sacred purpose imprinted, within our souls reminding us that we are never alone and that their presence has always been with us.

## *Awakening to Divine Love Humanity's Sacred Destiny*

As we align our hearts with this sacred purpose we become part of a shared journey of awakening. Every act of self-love every moment of compassion brings us closer to embodying the divine harmony of love and unity.

Humanity's ascension is deeply connected to the ascension of Earth Gaia as we grow within, we contribute to Gaia's healing and transformation. When we choose love over fear peace over conflict, we become channels of divine light anchoring these higher energies into Gaia herself. This spiritual evolution is not some distant ideal it is a living reality we can embrace in each moment.

## *Embracing Divine Love, The Birth right of Every Soul*

In the following pages I invite you to embrace the path to higher frequencies that is your destiny birthright. This journey begins within the sacred centre of your heart where soul and spirit meet as one.

Here in this quiet space your Guardian Angel and higher self, whisper timeless truths gently guiding you back to the light and purpose that have always been within you.

Through this heart-centred connection you gain access to deep wisdom and the unique role you play, in the unfolding masterpiece of creation. Humanity's collective ascension is our shared destiny a journey back to love wholeness and the eternal symphony each of us is here to play.

## *Remembering the Ancient Wisdom A Journey of the Soul's Purpose*

Each soul is a note or octave in the universal symphony a single beautiful sound. As Mena explained every soul carries a blueprint a sacred contract made with the Divine Creator. This contract holds our commitment to gather and return adding new harmonies to the celestial composition.

Sometimes we forget this purpose humanity can be influenced by dark forces that do not belong to the Creator's vision may follow paths of chaos and discord. While these dark forces sow disharmony the divine symphony resonates with light, peace, love, harmony laughter and joy, These beautiful qualities are the birth right of every soul always accessible waiting for us to reach out and reconnect.

## *Creating a Sacred Space and Altar – A Path to Divine Connection*

Take a moment to pause, breathe and settle into the comforting presence of your Guardian Angel. As we journey through this chapter together, we will explore the art of creating a sacred space and altar as acts of self-love, compassion and spiritual grounding.

In the fast-paced world we inhabit, dedicating a space to reconnect with your spirit is a gift to your soul. Your sacred altar is more than a physical arrangement of cherished objects; it is a living reflection of your inner world, an anchor of divine connection that bridges the realms of spirit and matter.

## 1: Preparing a Sacred Space for Angelic Healing

The foundation of all healing begins with nurturing the spiritual connection between your mind, body and spirit. This practice is an invitation to embrace, stillness and open your heart to the loving presence of your Guardian Angel. When you set aside intentional time for meditation and reconnection, you create a sanctuary where divine healing can flourish.

Focus on the joyful, heartfelt intention of crafting a space that feels sacred and meaningful in your life. Whether it is dedicating an entire room, lighting a single candle, to create a small altar each step becomes a loving act of devotion inviting your Guardian Angel, the gentle messenger of divine love, to draw near. When you enter this sacred space, you initiate a powerful energetic shift, building a bridge between your physical being and the higher realms of spiritual peace and light. In this haven, you are held in unconditional love, cherished and safe to open your heart fully to the profound love of the divine your sacred heart chamber.

Begin by choosing a quiet, comforting corner in your home where you can feel at ease and undisturbed. Let this place be one that naturally uplifts your spirit, illuminated by soft natural light and free of clutter. A clean and harmonious environment helps to foster a high-vibrational energy to welcome the angels. To further cleanse the space, gently waft the purifying smoke of white sage or other sacred herbs, while opening the windows to release any lingering negativity.

As you do this, visualise the space filling with light, love and peace, creating a cocoon of positivity and protection.

Invite your Guardian Angel with a heartfelt prayer, spoken from the depths of your soul:

"Beloved beautiful Guardian Angel, I welcome you into this sacred space. Please help me cleanse and bless this place, filling it with your divine light, infinite love and healing energy."

As you feel sense their loving presence, express your deep gratitude for their guidance and care.

Show reverence for this divine connection by lovingly maintaining the space, keeping it both physically clean and energetically vibrant. This small act of devotion honours not only your Guardian Angel but also your own sacred journey of healing and spiritual growth.

## 2: Creating a Sacred Altar

Crafting a personal altar is a profoundly kind and meaningful act one that transcends the simple arrangement of objects. It is an outward expression of your soul's inner truth, sanctuary where the sacred meets the everyday and where divine love flows freely. With your sacred space prepared you are now invited to create a heart-centred altar a sanctuary that reflects your inner world and deepens your connection with the divine and your Guardian Angel.

Personally, my life has been profoundly enriched by the creation of altars and spiritual spaces I hold close to my heart. As a child, I found pure joy in gathering shells, stones and other cherished objects as well as selecting favourite paintings that spoke to my soul. These early altars were simple yet deeply intuitive, reflecting the wonder and beauty I felt within. Over time, these small sanctuaries evolved into intentional spaces of devotion and love anchoring me to my innermost truths and strengthening my connection to the divine love and light.

Think of your altar as a refuge a sacred haven where peace, inspiration and stillness reside. It is both a mirror of your spiritual journey and a tender offering of love to yourself and the universe. Your altar becomes a tangible reminder that you are lovingly supported by your Guardian Angel and the sacred presence that encompasses all of life.

Ask yourself What stirs my heart? What objects hold deep meaning for me, reflecting my hopes, dreams and inner thoughts?

### 3: Grounding and Balancing Your Energy Centres

Creating a divine connection is profoundly enhanced by grounding and balancing your energy centres. This practice invites you into a sacred state where the nurturing energy of Gaia meets the transcendent love of the divine. As you embark on this process, visualise yourself as a strong, towering tree with roots that stretch deeply into the nourishing core of the Gaia. These roots anchor you, allowing you to draw up Earth's stable warm energy.

This grounding practice does not just connect you to the physical world but establishes a harmonious link between Gaia's ancient wisdom and the higher realms of divine spirit.

Try as best you can to imagine a warm golden light streaming down from the heavens, gently caressing the crown of your head. This light represents the divine spirit pure, compassionate and infinitely loving. As it flows into you, it moves with a gentle soothing, nurturing quality, washing over each of your energy centres chakras. Picture it is cascading down through your crown, illuminating each chakra in turn, filling your body with a serene warmth that dissolves tension and awakens peace. This flow of divine love energy revitalises you balancing and aligning your seven main chakras. Each energy centre begins to resonate in harmony glowing with vibrant, balanced energy.

The pure radiant energy infuses your body with divine spiritual unconditional love, healing and divine nourishment.

The warm, flowing pure energy gently unravels any stagnant energy or blocks, promoting inner clarity and an expansive sense of well-being. It is as if a river of light courses through you, carrying with its messages of divine wisdom and unconditional love. This state of connection strengthens your bond with your Guardian Angel, making their loving presence more tangible. The warmth you feel is not just an abstract concept; it is a living force that holds, comforts and uplifts you.

This technique is known as grounding into spirit as you continue to practice grounding and balancing your energy, you may notice subtle shifts. Your thoughts become more focused, your emotions steadier and your body more relaxed. This connection adopts not only spiritual growth but a profound inner peace that stays with you, even amidst life's challenges. It deepens your capacity to love and be loved, developing all your senses, opening you up to life's beauty with newfound meaning of divine love.

Grounding and balancing your energy centres are more than a technique; it is an act of loving kindness, devotion to yourself and to the divine love that sustains all of creation.

### 4: Reconnecting with Your Guardian Angel

Now that your altar is prepared and your energy balanced, it is time to intentionally reconnect with your Guardian Angel. Begin by sitting comfortably, placing your left hand over your higher heart and your right hand over your solar plexus. This hand position aligns you physically with the divine, creating a soothing connection between you and your Guardian Angel. Set a clear intention for reconnection, saying, "Dear Guardian Angel, I call upon your loving guidance. Please heal me on all levels and fill my being with your light." Allow yourself to feel the warmth of this connection as the energy of your Guardian Angel enfolds you. This practice is deeply transformative, bringing clarity and healing into your life as you open yourself to the divine guidance and protection that is always available. [full meditation reconnects with your Guardian angel chapter 10]. I recommend you self-record adding deeper bond.

### 5: Awakening the Divine Potential Within

Reconnecting with your Guardian Angel is a sacred journey that invites divine blessings into your life. As you nurture this bond, you awaken to the limitless love and wisdom within you. Each moment spent in communion with your Guardian Angel opens you to a sacred flow of peace, compassion and spiritual grace. Imagine stepping into a sanctuary where the compassion of Christ and the peace of Buddha reside. This sacred chamber within your heart allows divine love and wisdom to infuse your life, becoming a source of comfort insight and empowerment.

Your Guardian Angel is not only a guide, protector but a sacred teacher of the soul. They gently guide you to new depths of understanding, encouraging you to release old fears and see yourself through the loving eyes of the divine. Over time, this relationship with your Guardian Angel deepens your ability to see the beauty and worthiness within, helping you align with others who resonate with love and compassion for all beings.

### 6: Closing Your Sacred Space and Grounding Excessive Energy

After connecting with your Guardian Angel, remember to ground yourself and close your spiritual sacred space. Spiritual experiences, while uplifting, can leave you feeling detached or unbalanced. Grounding helps you anchor the divine insights and love you have received, bringing you back to the present with clarity and ease.

You might gently stretch, step outside, or place your hands on the Gaia, allowing nature's support to stabilise your energy. Simple, mindful actions ensure the divine energy stays with you, balanced and grounded.

When closing your sacred space, give thanks with a full heart for the love, wisdom and protection shared. Visualise your Guardian Angel returning to their place in the higher realms, yet trust their presence remains with you, guiding and protecting you as you move forward. With this final act of gratitude and respect, you seal the energy shared, bringing its blessings into your daily life.

## 7: Affirmations of Gratitude: Sacred Journaling

Writing down your thoughts and feelings is a powerful way to reconnect with your Guardian Angel. Through sacred journaling, you create space for divine guidance and deepen your spiritual awareness. Gratitude strengthens this sacred bond, inviting harmony, protection and love into your life.

By consciously expressing gratitude, you align yourself with higher vibrations, making it easier to receive angelic messages and trust in the unseen support surrounding you. Whether written daily or spoken aloud, these affirmations will help you nurture your connection and embrace the blessings of divine presence:

### *Affirmations of Gratitude for Your Guardian Angel*

*"I am grateful for the divine presence of my Guardian Angel, whose love, wisdom and protection guide me each day."*

*"I honour the sacred bridge between the physical and spiritual realms, knowing I am always supported on my journey."*

*"I am grounded, centred and balanced, carrying the radiant light of my Guardian Angel into every moment of my life."*

*"With an open heart, I receive the gentle guidance of my Guardian Angel and trust in the divine plan unfolding before me."*

*"Gratitude fills my soul as I recognise the signs, synchronicities and whispers of love from my Guardian Angel."*

As you engage in sacred journaling, allow these affirmations to flow through your words and intentions. The more you express appreciation, the more you cultivate an atmosphere of divine love, reassurance and peace. Your Guardian Angel is always near gently guiding you toward your highest good.

## *Divine Connection: A Journey of Awakening*

This spiritual act is a sacred bridge, a divine connection of trust, acceptance, forgiveness, guidance and surrender. It is a gentle yet powerful reminder of your inherent strength and self-worth. As you honour and reflect upon your devotion, you deepen your connection to the divine within you.

Whether you call upon God, Goddess, or the infinite Divine Consciousness, this presence is pure unconditional love and available to all who seek it

My heart overflows with joy in sharing this wisdom, knowing that with each visit to your sacred space, your awareness expands aligning you ever more closely with your true purpose.

Carry forward the love, grace and serenity found here into your daily life, resting in the truth that you are deeply cherished, eternally supported and always guided. As you take each step, allow yourself to fully experience the journey, not just with your mind but through the depths of your heart and soul. Sink into the present moment, feeling each breath as a gentle embrace of life itself. Reconnecting with your Guardian Angel is reconnecting with your true authentic self.

*Photograph of my Altar*

CHAPTER 2

# The Chakras – A Spiritual Journey

Imagine your body as a delicate instrument, finely tuned to the energies that flow within and around you. Ancient teachings reveal that within each of us lie seven radiant wheels of energy known as chakras, which hold the keys to our physical, emotional and spiritual harmony. Just as a melody becomes dissonant when an instrument is out of tune, so too can our lives feel unbalanced when our chakras are blocked or misaligned. This chapter invites you on a journey into the captivating world of energy within and around the body including crystals energy frequencies and vibration.

## *The Aura as a protective shield*

Let us explore the origins, meanings and profound impact of the aura on the mind, body and spirit. Gaining a deeper understanding of these energy centres opens the door to self-discovery, spiritual growth and a sense of inner peace. Embracing self-healing and balance you can learn to attune yourself to the colours, crystals and energies that promote a vibrant, healthy and spiritually aligned life.

The aura is a radiant multilayered field of energy that surrounds every living being. It acts as a dynamic and protective energy field often perceived as a multi-coloured glow. This energetic field reflects your overall well-being including your physical, emotional, mental and spiritual states.

Each layer of the aura corresponds to a specific aspect of your being. When the layers are balanced the aura facilitates the smooth flow of energy, shields you from external stress and negativity and supports holistic wellness. The concept of energy centres such as chakras further enriches our understanding of how the aura integrates with physical, mental, emotional and spiritual systems.

If you can have your aura photographed, often available at mind-body-spirit events, I highly recommend it. It is truly fascinating to witness. Aura imagining also known as kirlian photography, which captures electrical coronal discharges around objects, provides a visual representation of the energy field.

While it does not directly depict the aura, this technique offers insight into the subtle and interconnected energy systems that support harmony and balance in living beings.

As a clairvoyant, I have observed the auras of individuals suffering from chronic illnesses, burdened by toxic medications, or weakened by addictions to substances such as smoking, alcohol, or drugs. In these cases, their auric and etheric bodies often reveal dark holes of varying sizes and depths energetic wounds that leave them increasingly vulnerable. Sadly, the larger and deeper these holes, the more susceptible they become too negative energies, which infiltrate the body, cloud the mind and distort perception.

An energy parasite is a non-physical entity or force that feeds on a person's life force, often attaching itself to those who are energetically depleted, emotionally vulnerable, or spiritually unprotected. These parasitic energies can take many forms persistent negative thought patterns, intrusive emotions, or even external entities that suck energy from the auric field. They thrive in low-vibrational states, exploiting emotional distress, fear and exhaustion to deepen their hold.

Those who are chronically stressed, emotionally drained, or lacking strong energetic boundaries such as empaths, caregivers, and individuals battling addiction are particularly susceptible. The symptoms of energy parasitism often manifest as chronic fatigue, brain fog, emotional instability, heightened anxiety, and a profound sense of being "drained" after interactions with certain people or environments. If left unaddressed, prolonged energy depletion can sever one's connection to their higher self, making spiritual clarity and renewal increasingly difficult. Yet, depleted auras are not limited to those suffering from addiction.

I have witnessed many individuals including habitual substance users and those experiencing deep spiritual exhaustion struggle with similar energetic weaknesses.

Those who are too overwhelmed to reconnect with nature often find themselves unknowingly inviting energy parasites, which drain their vitality and leave them feeling empty and disconnected.

This is especially true for empaths, highly intelligent and deeply compassionate souls who give so much of themselves to others. While their kindness is a rare and beautiful gift, constant energy depletion without the balance of self-care and loving-kindness toward themselves can leave them exposed to emotional exhaustion, spiritual disconnection and external negative influences.

However, no one is broken. The soul remains whole, even when aspects of it feel lost. Trauma, exhaustion and negative influences may create a sense of fragmentation, leaving a person confused, detached, or uncertain of their path. Healing is always possible. Beneath the weariness, we are loved, we are accepted and we are never truly separate from our wholeness. Remembering this truth is essential when we trust in our own ability to heal, we begin to restore balance, reclaim our energy and step back into alignment with our highest self.

One of the most powerful ways to restore this balance is through practicing loving-kindness both toward ourselves and others. True healing is not just about setting energetic boundaries or shielding ourselves from negativity; it is also about cultivating compassion, patience and forgiveness. When we extend love to ourselves, we strengthen our inner light, making it harder for lower energies to take hold. When we extend love to others, we elevate the collective frequency, creating ripples of healing that reach far beyond ourselves.

## *True Story of Hope*

I was reminded of this truth one day when I met Stephen, a young man crumbled on the pavement outside my healing sanctuary.

His skin was grey, his body thin and shaking, his aura tattered and torn by years of alcohol addiction. His eyes, once bright with the spark of life, were now clouded with sorrow and exhaustion.

He was completely lost, his soul fragmented by years of suffering. In his addiction, he had unknowingly given parts of himself away to dark energies forces that had taken hold of his mind, whispering despair, feeding his dependence and draining his will to live.

Stephen was not just physically weak he was mentally and emotionally broken, desperate to escape reality. Alcohol had become his refuge, a way to silence the pain, to numb himself from the world, to disappear. He drank to forget, to lose himself in the haze of oblivion, to block out the unbearable weight of his own existence. Each blackout, each lost night, took him further from himself. The deeper he fell, the harder it became to remember who he had once been.

With quiet desperation, he lifted his head and asked for help. In that moment, I felt the presence of his Guardian Angel, guiding me toward him. Though his body was weak, the act of reaching out signified a shift an opening, however small, for healing to begin. I knelt beside him and placed a piece of amethyst in his trembling hands, programming it with the intention of alleviating his pain and easing his cravings. It was a small act, but a meaningful one. The crystal carried an energy of protection, clarity and transformation and I knew it would serve as a beacon of light in his darkest moments.

Stephen began receiving weekly spiritual healing and with each session, his aura grew stronger.

The holes in his etheric body started to mend, his energy became steadier and the darkness that once clung to him slowly faded. As his spirit reawakened, so did his determination.

He not only overcame his addiction but also found a renewed sense of purpose he trained as an ambulance worker, dedicating his life to saving others in need.

Years later, Stephen walked back into my healing sanctuary, this time he was not the broken man I had first met. His eyes were bright, his energy strong.

By his side stood his young family his loving partner and their child. He was alcohol-free, holding down a stable job and living with purpose. He was happy, present, fully engaged in life.

The man who had once tried to disappear had now found himself. He was no longer running from his pain; he had transformed it into strength, wisdom and compassion. He was at last, living his best life.

Without conscious replenishment, individuals may suffer from poor sleep, chronic fatigue, persistent anxiety, or an increasing sense of detachment from their inner wisdom. True healing requires more than just rest it calls for a deliberate restoration of the etheric body through grounding in nature, strengthening energetic boundaries, realigning with higher vibrational energies and embracing the practice of loving-kindness as a path to deep spiritual well-being. Most importantly, it requires self-trust. Trusting in one's own capacity for healing is the key to full health and wholeness.

Stephen's journey is a testament to this truth when we ask for help, when we believe in our own ability to heal and when we are willing to receive love and guidance, transformation is always possible. No matter how lost we may feel, we are never beyond healing. The light within us is eternal it only waits for us to turn toward it once more.

For guidance on protecting and strengthening the etheric body, refer to Chapter 10: *Full Channelled Chakra Meditation*.

## *The layers of the aura include:*

**Physical Body:** The innermost layer is the physical body which is the tangible visible part of us. This layer represents our physical health, vitality and how we take care of ourselves.

Self-love is imperative to nourish your physical body with healthy foods, rest, exercise and self-care. A strong healthy physical body supports all the other layers of your aura.

**Etheric Body:** The next layer is the etheric body which mirrors your physical body in a finer energy form. It is often seen as a blueprint or a web of energy that keeps the physical body strong. This is where healing begins and by keeping your physical body healthy you support the strength of your etheric layer.

Think of it as your body's energetic defence system, keeping it strong through good health ensures protection.

Emotional Body: Your emotional body holds your feelings, moods and how you express emotions. If you are feeling joy, love or peace this layer will glow brightly. When you are holding onto anger, sadness, or anxiety the emotional body can become cloudy or dim. It is important to allow yourself to feel and release emotions in a healthy way through journaling, talking to someone or meditation so your emotional body can stay light and balanced.

**Mental Body:** The mental body is where your thoughts, beliefs and attitudes reside. This layer is influenced by the quality of your thoughts. Positive loving thoughts help it shine while negative critical or anxious thinking can weigh it down. Practicing compassionate self-love, staying in the present moment, mindfulness, positive affirmations and focusing on positive thoughts can keep this layer clear helping you feel mentally sharp and optimistic.

**Astral Body:** The astral body is connected to your capacity for love and relationships. It is a higher level of emotional energy that connects you to others. When this layer is balanced, you feel deeply connected to yourself and the people around you radiate love and compassion.

Spending time with loved ones, practicing forgiveness and cultivating gratitude strengthen this layer making your relationships more fulfilling and heart centred.

**Celestial Body:** The celestial body is the seat of your higher consciousness and intuition. It is the place where you connect with your Guardian Angel, spiritual guides and the divine. When this layer is healthy you feel spiritually aware and in tune with the universe. Meditation, prayer and practices like gratitude help you access this part of yourself deepening your spiritual connection and wisdom.

**Causal Body**: The causal body or higher spiritual body is the outermost layer representing the link between your soul and the infinite universe. This is where you experience the ultimate connection to divine consciousness and universal love.

Keeping this layer strong helps you live in alignment with your highest self and the flow of the universe.

## *The aura and the seven chakras*

I see the aura as a beautiful kaleidoscope of colours, constantly moving and changing. For me, this is part of being clairvoyant, it's how I perceive energy. The aura is a field of energy that surrounds every living being. It's not just one solid colour; it's made up of many layers and shifting shades that reflect our thoughts, emotions, physical state and spiritual well-being.

The aura and the chakras are deeply connected. Each chakra is an energy centre within the body and together, they influence the colours and flow of the aura. When our chakras are balanced, the aura appears vibrant and clear. When we're stressed, unwell, or emotionally off-balance, the aura can become dull or heavy.

To me, the aura is like an energetic fingerprint, uniquely yours and always communicating something about your inner world.

**Root Chakra (Base of Spine)** The Root Chakra is the foundation of your energy system. It connects you to the earth and your sense of security. When balanced you feel grounded, safe and supported in life. Eating nourishing foods and spending time in nature can strengthen this chakra.

**Sacral Chakra (Lower Abdomen)** The Sacral Chakra governs your creativity, emotions and sensuality. When open you feel joyful, enthusiastic and connected to your desires.

Creative expression and honouring your emotions are key to balancing this chakra.

**Solar Plexus Chakra (Upper Abdomen**) The Solar Plexus is your centre of personal power and confidence. A balanced Solar Plexus helps you feel empowered, in control and confident in your decisions. Practicing self-discipline and setting clear boundaries strengthens this energy centre.

**Heart Chakra (Centre of Chest)** The Heart Chakra is the bridge between your physical and spiritual self. It is the source of love, compassion and emotional balance. When your heart chakra is open you feel love for yourself and others and you experience deep emotional healing. Acts of kindness, forgiveness and self-love nourish this chakra.

**Throat Chakra (Throat)** The Throat Chakra governs communication, self-expression and speaking your truth. When balanced you communicate clearly, honestly and with love. Practicing open, honest conversations and expressing your authentic self helps keep this chakra healthy.

**Third Eye Chakra (Forehead)** The Third Eye Chakra is your centre of intuition, inner wisdom and perception. It allows you to see beyond the physical world and trust your inner knowing.

Practices like meditation and visualisation help activate and balance this chakra connecting you to your higher self and intuition.

**Crown Chakra (Top of Head)** The Crown Chakra is your connection to divine consciousness, the universe and your spiritual self. A balanced Crown Chakra brings a sense of inner peace, spiritual connection and enlightenment. Meditation, prayer and spiritual reflection help open this energy centre linking you to the divine.

Your aura and chakras play a crucial role in your overall well-being. When these energy centres are balanced and aligned, you experience a sense of vitality, inner harmony and connection on physical, emotional, mental and spiritual levels. Maintaining this balance supports your body's natural ability to heal, shields you from stress and negativity and promotes a state of overall well-being.

When energy flows freely through your aura and chakras, you feel stable and secure in both your body and your life. Emotionally, you experience greater resilience and balance; mentally, your thoughts become clearer and more focused.

You also develop a deeper connection with others, cultivate spiritual awareness and align more closely with your soul's true purpose. By caring for and nurturing your aura and chakras, you create a life filled with love, health, joy and fulfilment, allowing you to live in alignment with your highest potential.

## *Understanding the Chakras*

In the Western world, chakras are not acknowledged within mainstream medical science. The idea of energy centres within the body is often regarded as metaphysical rather than physical, as they cannot be measured or observed like a pulse or blood flow.

While there is widespread acceptance of the body's electrical activity, such as the heart's rhythm or the brain's neural impulses, the idea of chakras as energy hubs remains outside conventional medical frameworks.

While the understanding of chakras may not align with Western medical frameworks, many find value in these concepts as part of a broader approach to health and spirituality. Whether viewed as metaphorical or literal, chakras offer a framework for exploring the connection between mind, body and spirit and for fostering balance and harmony within us.

There are numerous chakras within our four-body system, but here we will focus on the seven primary chakras.

Rooted in Indian Ayurvedic principles, these energy centres are intricately connected to our well-being. Each chakra aligns with a specific location in the body and resonates with organs, colours, planets and birth signs, reflecting its unique qualities and connection to the natural world. These energy centres act as pathways for the life force that nourishes and sustains the mind, body and soul.

When working with the chakras, approach this sacred practice with loving kindness and gentle awareness. Give yourself the time and space to explore without rushing or overthinking. This is not a process of intellectualising but an invitation to feel, sense and notice the subtle shifts in your energy. Regular practice is the key to staying present in the moment, fostering a deeper connection with your physical body and the energy that flows through you.

## *The Essence of Energy and Spiritual Balance*

As you chant, lovingly call upon the support of your Guardian Angel and personal team of spiritual guides, inviting their presence to assist in balancing, opening and closing each energy centre. Allow yourself to experience this process intuitively, focusing on the gentle sensations and changes within your energy field. Trust that even the smallest shifts hold profound significance and contribute to your overall harmony.

This introduction is not intended to be a comprehensive explanation but rather a heartfelt foundation for exploring the chakras and their profound potential to bring balance, peace and presence into your life.

## *The Seven Chakras and Their Vibrational frequencies and Sounds*

### **Root Chakra (Muladhara):**

Location: Base of the spine

Element: Earth

Colour: Red

Planet: Saturn

Organs: Bones, legs, feet, large intestine

Chant: LAM

Energy: Grounding, security, stability

The root chakra forms the foundation of your energetic system, representing survival, grounding and connection to the earth. Chanting LAM activates the root chakra, fostering stability and security.

Visualise a warm red glow at the base of your spine as you chant, grounding yourself in the earth's nurturing energy. The deep resonance of LAM reminds you of your innate connection to the physical world, helping release fear and embrace courage.

### Sacral Chakra (Svadhisthana):

Location: Lower abdomen

Element: Water

Colour: Orange

Planet: Jupiter

Organs: Reproductive system, bladder, kidneys

Chant: VAM

Energy: Creativity, pleasure, emotional flow

The sacral chakra governs creativity, sensuality and emotional well-being. Chanting VAM awakens its energy, encouraging emotional clarity and creative flow. Visualise an orange glow in your lower abdomen as you chant, allowing emotions to move freely like water. VAM releases emotional blockages, inspiring joy and passion and inviting you to embrace life's creative possibilities.

### Solar Plexus Chakra (Manipura):

Location: Above the navel

Element: Fire

Colour: Yellow

Planet: Mars

Organs: Stomach, pancreas, liver

Chant: RAM

Energy: Confidence, willpower, personal power

The solar plexus chakra is the centre of personal power, confidence and motivation.

Chanting RAM activates the fire within, igniting courage and determination. Visualise a radiant yellow light in your abdomen as you chant, fuelling your inner strength. The vibration of RAM empowers purposeful action and manifests clarity and confidence.

**Heart Chakra (Anahata):**

| | |
|---|---|
| Location: | Centre of the chest |
| Element: | Air |
| Colour: | Green or pink |
| Planet: | Venus |
| Organs: | Heart, lungs, circulatory system |
| Chant: | YAM |
| Energy: | Love, compassion, harmony |

The heart chakra is the bridge between the physical and spiritual realms, symbolising love and compassion. Chanting YAM opens the heart to unconditional kindness and empathy. Visualise a soothing green light radiating from your chest as you chant, dissolving grief and bitterness. YAM fosters harmonious relationships and a compassionate connection to others.

**Throat Chakra (Vishuddha):**

| | |
|---|---|
| Location: | Throat |
| Element: | Ether |
| Colour: | Blue |
| Planet: | Mercury |
| Organs: | Throat, thyroid, vocal cords |
| Chant: | HAM |
| Energy: | Communication, self-expression, truth |

The throat chakra governs communication and authenticity. Chanting HAM clears blockages, allowing you to speak your truth with clarity and compassion. Visualise a vibrant blue light at your throat as you chant, opening pathways for authentic expression. HAM fosters confidence in your voice and invites truthful communication.

### Third Eye Chakra (Ajna):

Location: Between the eyebrows

Element: Light

Colour: Indigo

Planet: Moon

Organs: Brain, eyes, nervous system

Chant: OM

Energy: Intuition, insight, spiritual wisdom. The third eye chakra represents intuition and spiritual awareness. Chanting OM aligns you with universal wisdom and creation.

Visualise a deep indigo light glowing between your eyebrows as you chant, opening your mind's eye and expanding perception. OM deepens insight and connects you to the infinite truth of your being. OM is considered the primordial sound of the universe, representing the vibration of creation itself.

When chanted, it resonates through the body and mind, aligning you with the flow of universal energy.

In relation to the third eye chakra, also known as the Ajna chakra, OM is particularly powerful, as it stimulates intuition, inner wisdom and spiritual awareness.

The third eye chakra, located between the eyebrows, governs perception beyond the physical senses. It is the centre of insight, imagination and higher consciousness. Chanting OM while focusing on this chakra helps to clear mental fog, heighten intuition and deepen your connection to the unseen dimensions of existence. The vibration of OM acts as a tuning fork, harmonising your energy with divine knowledge and opening pathways to expanded consciousness.

As you chant, visualise a deep indigo light radiating from your third eye, growing brighter with each vibration. This light symbolises clarity, wisdom and the ability to see beyond illusion. With regular practice, chanting OM can enhance your ability to trust your intuition, recognise synchronicities and perceive the interconnectedness of all things. It serves as a bridge between the physical and spiritual realms, guiding you toward enlightenment and the infinite truth of your being.

**Crown Chakra (Sahasrara):**

Location: Top of the head
Element: Cosmic energy
Colour: Violet or white
Planet: Uranus
Organs: Brain, nervous system
Chant: Shanti OM
Energy: Spiritual connection, unity, enlightenment

The crown chakra symbolises spiritual unity and divine connection. Chanting Shanti OM invokes peace and universal harmony. Visualise a violet or white light radiating from the top of your head as you chant, aligning with cosmic energy.

The resonance of Shanti OM fosters serenity and oneness.

## *The Healing Power of Chanting*

Chanting these sacred sounds awakens the energies within each chakra, bringing balance to your physical, mental, emotional spiritual bodies. This practice reminds of our divine essence, anchoring in the truth that we are deeply interconnected with all of creation.

Through the healing power of sound and vibration, we embrace harmony, love and unity.

Let your chakra practice be a reminder that you are both a vessel and a participant in the flow of divine energy.

Trust the process, honour yourself and celebrate the profound beauty of balancing your energy system. As you continue this journey, know that you are held in a sacred space of love and compassion, supported by your Guardian Angel, the divine and your own inner light.

## *Crystals and Colours: Tools for Chakra Healing*

Crystals hold a unique place in the connection between humanity, the rhythm of Earth, and the higher frequencies of divine creation. They are far more than beautiful stones, they are gifts from nature, infused with the Earth's ancient wisdom. When attuned with loving intention and guided by your Guardian Angel, you can begin to experience how these sacred tools resonate with your own unique frequency.

Each crystal carries a vibration, a quiet yet profound frequency that aligns with the rhythms of Earth itself. When held, worn, or placed with intention, these natural treasures become powerful allies gently supporting us as we align with our highest potential.

Personally, I think of crystals as trusted friends. Each one can be programmed to align with our intentions and support our purpose. Their vibrant colours and unique energies have guided me in healing emotional wounds, opening my heart to compassion, balancing my energy, and helping me stay grounded.

They speak directly to our subtle energy centres the chakras helping to clear blockages and restore the flow of *prana*, the vital life force that flows through all living beings.

Whether a crystal finds its way into your pocket, your home, or your heart, it brings with it a unique ability to guide, nurture, and heal.

## *Crystals and Chakra Energy*

As you embark on your journey with crystals, you'll discover how their vibrant colours and healing properties connect with your chakras. Each crystal has the potential to amplify your energy and intentions, acting as a bridge between the physical and spiritual realms.

When combined with mindful intention, the energy of crystals can open powerful pathways to healing and growth. These sacred stones remind us that the beauty of the Earth is always available to uplift and inspire. Let yourself connect with their quiet power, and allow them to guide you toward a life of harmony, love, and divine connection.

Each chakra resonates with specific crystals and colours, offering gentle tools to restore balance and clear emotional blockages:

- **Root Chakra:** Red Jasper or Hematite provide grounding energy, offering stability and strength.
- **Sacral Chakra:** Carnelian or Orange Calcite ignite joy, creativity, and emotional flow.
- **Solar Plexus Chakra:** Yellow Calcite, Citrine, or Yellow Jasper help reclaim personal power and confidence.
- **Heart Chakra:** Rose Quartz or Green Aventurine open the heart to love, compassion, and healing.
- **Throat Chakra:** Blue Lace Agate or Aquamarine encourage clear, authentic communication.
- **Third Eye Chakra:** Amethyst or Purple Fluorite enhance intuition and spiritual insight.
- **Crown Chakra:** Clear Quartz or Selenite connect us to divine consciousness and enlightenment.

When placed on or near the corresponding energy centres, these stones vibrate in harmony with the chakras, encouraging the free flow of *prana*, and gently supporting emotional and spiritual healing.

## *Crystal and Divine Healing*

Crystals have long held a place of reverence in my life. To me, they are sacred tools carrying the unique frequencies of the Earth. Each crystal is imbued with its own vibration an energetic imprint of Earth's wisdom and resonates with different aspects of our journey.

These remarkable gems act as amplifiers, intensifying our intentions and harmonising with our energy. They form a bridge between us, the angelic realm, and the divine.

Through personal experience, I've come to see crystals as more than beautiful stones. They are companions on the spiritual path offering healing, clarity, and inner peace. Crafted by nature, they uplift the spirit, align us with our highest selves, and deepen our connection to our Guardian Angels.

## *Programming and Working with Crystals*

With loving intention and guidance from our Guardian Angel we have the ability to programme crystals to elevate the energy in our homes and sacred spaces, creating atmospheres of peace and harmony. Support our physical mental health and that of our pets. Thoughtfully arranged crystals absorb and transmute electromagnetic frequencies, filling the environment with serene, high-vibrational energy that nurtures emotional and mental well-being.

Choosing crystals intuitively with guidance from your higher self and Guardian Angel helps you align your space with your intentions. Creating a crystal grid, a geometric arrangement of stones, can amplify energy for healing, protection, or abundance.

Carrying a small crystal in your pocket or purse is a comforting way to stay grounded throughout the day.

My home has become a sanctuary for crystals. They rest on every windowsills in every room by each bed, and even in the bathroom.

Meditating with them has become a daily sacred practice, allowing me to connect with divine frequencies, my higher self, and the loving presence of my Guardian Angel. Holding a crystal or placing it on a chakra during meditation aligns its healing properties with my intention.

For example, black tourmaline provides grounding and stability when I feel anxious, while rose quartz fosters self-love and compassion. During meditation, the crystal's energy harmonises with my intention, guiding me to a peaceful, centred state.

Wearing crystals as jewellery, necklaces, bracelets, rings keeps their healing vibration close, offering subtle support throughout the day. Remember to physically and spiritually cleanse them as they become depleted in energy

## *Intuitive Selection and Ritual*

Selecting a crystal is a deeply personal and intuitive process. Trust your inner knowing and let your heart guide you to the stone that resonates with your energy.

Once chosen, you can program your crystal to amplify its energy. I hold the crystal in my hands, feel its weight and subtle vibration, and gently cleanse it under running water. Then, speaking aloud, I invite my Guardian Angel to assist:

"Dear beautiful Guardian Angel, please infuse this crystal with divine love and purpose."

As I speak, I visualise the crystal radiating light, attuned to my intention. This sacred moment becomes a partnership between myself, the crystal, and the angelic realm.

## *Cleansing and Honouring Your Crystals*

Caring for your crystals ensures their energy flows harmoniously. Many crystals thrive in sunlight or moonlight, which purifies and recharges their essence.

I often place mine by the window or outside to absorb the light, sometimes asking my Guardian Angel to bless them with divine protection.

One of my most memorable experiences was with a yellow calcite. After a long, emotionally draining clinic day, I could sense that its energy had diminished, it felt tired, as though it had been absorbing negativity on my behalf. I thanked it, then placed it in the soil to rest and renew. Months later, I rediscovered it glowing with vibrant energy, ready to serve once more. That moment reminded me of the natural cycles of giving, receiving, and restoration that connect us all.

## *Living in Partnership with Crystals*

Crystals carry distinct qualities that speak to many aspects of healing and spiritual growth:

- ❖ **Amethyst** calms the mind, protects against negativity, and fosters intuition.
- ❖ **Rose Quartz** heals emotional wounds, nurtures self-love, and opens the heart.
- ❖ **Clear Quartz** amplifies energy, enhances clarity, and serves as the "master healer."
- ❖ **Black Tourmaline** provides grounding and shields against negative influences.

Each stone is a gentle guide, walking beside you as you grow.

Through my own journey, I've experienced how crystals serve as channels for divine energy, especially in connection to my Guardian Angel. For instance, carrying rose quartz while repeating the affirmation, *"I am worthy of love and compassion,"* creates a profound sense of support and self-love.

## *A Story from Beyond the Veil*

One day, while walking along the high street, a green aventurine tumble stone caught my eye.

I picked it up and gently asked, *"Are you meant for me?"* The answer was clear: *"No, the lady behind you."*

I turned and saw a refined woman walking briskly toward the crystals. Guided by my Guardian Angel, I said, "Excuse me, you dropped something beautiful." She looked puzzled, but paused. I added, "This green aventurine is a powerful healer for the heart. You've lost someone dear and they want you to have it."

Tears welled in her eyes as she picked up the stone and walked away. She didn't say thank you, but her husband in spirit did, telling me it was their 30th wedding anniversary.

## *A Closing Blessing*

As you come to the end of this chapter, I invite you to pause. Let your Guardian angel guide you toward choosing crystal. Hold a crystal in your hands and feel the gentle energy flowing through your chakras and aura. Open your mind to as you connect with the thought of being one with divine creation.

With each step toward balance, you awaken to your truest, most authentic self, embraced by the love of your Guardian Angel and the wisdom of the universe.

Let your journey with crystals continue, with light, love, and endless possibilities.

# *7 Main energy Centres Chakra's*

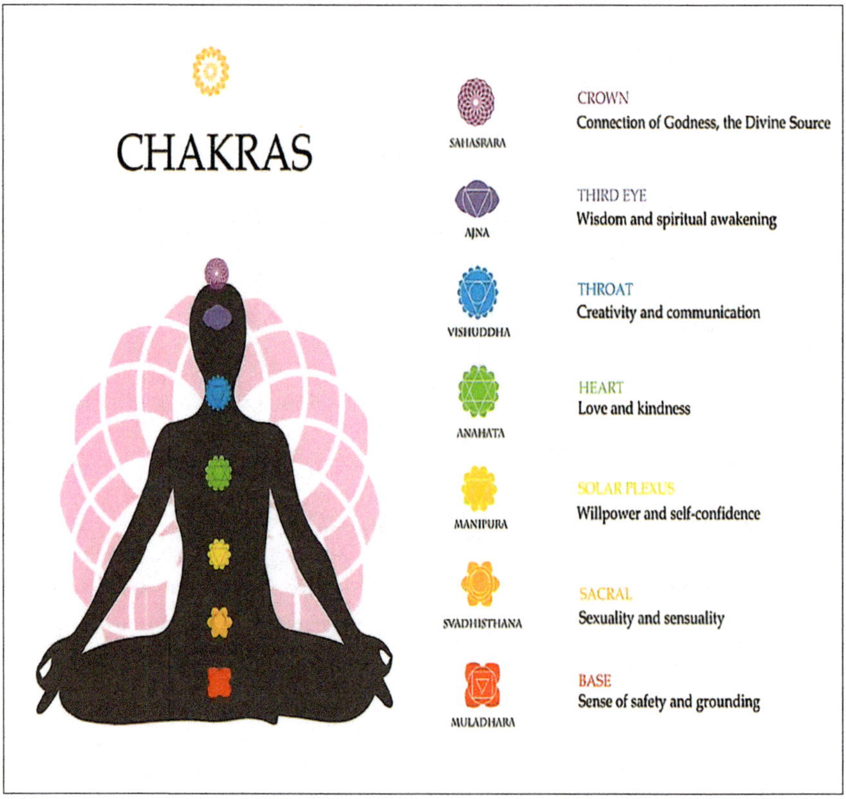

CHAPTER 3

# Sacred Geometry, Numerology, and Reconnection with Guardian Angels

I have always been fascinated by sacred architecture and the monuments of the ancients. There was something about the man echo, a pull that I couldn't explain. When I stood before these structures, I felt a strange familiarity, as if I had been there before. A doubt lingered at the edges of my mind. Was it simply my imagination? Or was there something more?

Mena, my Guardian Angel, often came to me in dreams and meditations, revealing glimpses of past lives. At first, I struggled to believe them visions of places I had never seen, lives I had never lived yet the emotions were so real they left me breathless. Could I trust what I was being shown? Or was I clinging to illusions, seeking meaning where there was none?

In moments of hesitation, Mena's presence would surround me like a quiet certainty.

"Trust what you feel," she would whisper, her voice neither demanding nor forceful, but patient, knowing. "You are remembering because you are meant to. There is a lesson in what you see."

And so, I began to understand: these glimpses were not just memories. In the stillness of our souls, we all seek a connection to something greater, an unspoken assurance that we are part of a divine design. It is within this sacred search that the universe speaks to us, not in words but in the silent language of light. It reaches beyond reason into the very essence of our being, guiding us, healing us, teaching us. When we listen, truly listen, we awaken to the wisdom that has always been there, waiting for us to remember.

## Vibrational Communication

The Language of Light resonates beyond the boundaries of human speech, encompassing sacred geometry, numerology and the subtle vibrations that align our souls with higher consciousness. This energetic language carries the essence of the divine, connecting us with the universe and our Guardian Angels. Through the shapes of nature, the glow of celestial patterns, or the harmonious repetition of angel numbers, we are called to recognise the spiritual codes embedded in our existence.

Timeless, recorded through all cultures in ancient history, and understood intuitively, the Language of Light is believed to be the original expression of creation. Through light codes, visual symbols, sound frequencies, or chants, we experience a spiritual activation that nurtures personal growth and healing, enhancing our connection to higher consciousness.

## Healing and Transformation

Engaging with the Language of Light through meditation, visualisation, or sound can clear energetic blockages and elevate our frequency. These practices often evoke feelings of peace, clarity, and emotional release as they harmonise the energetic body. The beauty of this sacred language is seen in the natural world, from the dance of sunlight on leaves to the symmetrical elegance of a snowflake, each holding divine codes that resonate with the soul.

Highly attuned individuals access this language through training and practice, interpreting the energies from higher realms as insights or visions that defy conventional speech and resonate with the spirit.

## Sacred Geometry: The Blueprint of Creation

Sacred geometry is the silent language of the divine, of all existence. It is the architecture of the universe, manifesting in the spirals of shells the branches of trees and their roots, the perfect formation of petals on flowers, the movement of galaxies, and the proportions of the human body. The Golden Ratio and the Fibonacci sequence, discovered and studied by Leonardo Fibonacci, reveal the mathematical perfection found in nature, art and even the sacred monuments of the ancients.

From the towering pyramids of Egypt to the intricate temples of the Mayans, from the wisdom of Mesopotamian scholars to the philosophies of ancient Greece, these civilisations all understood that geometry was more than just form, it was meaning, a bridge between the material and the spiritual divine. The Flower of Life, found across cultures and faiths is a symbol of creation itself, a blueprint of existence that speaks to the unity of all things. It appears in religious structures across the world, echoing the understanding that divine spiritual wisdom is universal beyond borders or beliefs.

Leonardo da Vinci's studies of the Vitruvian Man, sometimes seen as the Aquarian Man. A symbol of enlightenment and the unfolding of human potential demonstrates how the same sacred ratios are reflected within us. We are quite literally part of the same design that governs the stars, the oceans, and the breath we take.

Mena, my Guardian Angel, once whispered to me:

"Look beyond what is seen and you will understand. The messengers of God are in all that is."

And so, I began to see the patterns not just in stone and scripture but in the rhythm of life itself. Sacred geometry is not merely shapes and numbers; it is the very breath of creation the silent signature of the Divine written into everything that exists.

When we embrace this wisdom we attune ourselves to the cosmic order, aligning our spirit with the unseen forces that guide and uplift us. These sacred patterns remind us that we are held in divine harmony, where love and knowledge are the essence of our reality. Meditating on them is not just an act of reflection, it is a way of remembering who we truly are.

## *Angelic Numbers: Messages from the Divine Encoded in Repetition*

When you join up the dots of humanity's history it all makes sense all cultures faiths resonate with love and light. Angelic numbers are sequences that often appear in our lives with a frequency that feels far beyond mere coincidence.

These numbers, whether seen on clocks, license plates, phone numbers, receipts, or even pages in books, are a form of communication from Guardian Angels. Their presence serves as gentle guidance, offering insights and reassurance as we navigate life's journeys. They appear with intention, especially during moments when we seek encouragement, need confirmation, or yearn for a gentle nudge to stay on course. Below are some of the most recognised angelic numbers and their meanings. Angelic numbers are sequences that often appear in our lives with a frequency that feels far beyond mere coincidence.

## *The Meaning Behind Angel Numbers*

Each angel number carries its own unique energy and meaning, acting as a subtle message designed to help us feel supported, protected and aligned with our purpose. Noticing these patterns and opening our hearts to their significance, we develop a deeper relationship with the universe. This connection allows us to sense its wisdom and love gently guiding us toward greater understanding and fulfilment.

### 111: New Beginnings and Manifestation

When you see 111, it's a powerful reminder to stay mindful of your thoughts. This number signifies that you're in a period of heightened manifesting energy, where your thoughts are quickly becoming reality. Your angels are gently asking you to focus on positive intentions, new beginnings, or taking a step toward a dream. Seeing 111 is an invitation to align your thoughts and actions with what you truly want, as the universe is actively working to support your desires.

### 222: Sign of Balance and Harmony

The number 222 is a sign of balance, encouraging you to trust the process and have faith that everything is unfolding in divine timing. It often appears when you are in a period of growth or waiting, reminding you to be patient and trust that you're exactly where you need to be. This number reassures you that balance and harmony will soon restore themselves in your life, helping you to stay calm centred and balanced.

### 333: Support from Divine Beings

When you see 333, it's a message from ascended masters and divine beings, reassuring you of their presence and offering guidance. This number signals that you're not alone and that spiritual helpers are nearby, ready to assist you. Seeing 333 is an encouragement to call on their support, trust in their guidance and have faith in the steps you are taking.

### 444: Angelic Protection and Stability

The number 444 is a powerful symbol of angelic protection. It often appears during times of uncertainty, difficulty, or change. This number reassures you that you are safe and supported by your Guardian Angels, who are closely watching over you. 444 is a reminder that you're never alone and it encourages you to stand strong, knowing you are protected by divine forces.

### 555: Embracing Change and Transformation Seeing

555 is a message that change is on the horizon, often in ways that will lead to growth and transformation. This number encourages you to let go of what no longer serves you and to embrace new possibilities with an open heart. The angels want you to know that change, even when challenging, is part of your soul's journey, bringing you closer to your true purpose.

**666: Reconnection and Self-Reflection**

Though often misunderstood, 666 in the context of angel numbers is a reminder to reconnect with balance and focus on nurturing your inner self. It encourages you to reassess where you might have been, to focus on material concerns and to realign with your spiritual path. This number is a call to listen to your intuition and bring harmony back into your thoughts and actions.

**777: Spiritual Alignment and Divine Guidance**

Seeing 777 is a confirmation that you are on the right spiritual path. This number is a profound reminder that you're aligned with your higher purpose and that divine energies are guiding you. When you notice 777, you may feel a sense of peace, as though you're receiving a gentle acknowledgment from the universe that you are exactly where you're meant to be.

**888: Abundance and Financial Prosperity**

The number 888 is a powerful symbol of abundance, often associated with financial blessings and success. This number tells you that the universe is supporting your material and financial goals,and it encourages you to continue putting positive energy into your dreams. Seeing 888 may signal that rewards are on their way or that you're moving into a cycle of greater prosperity.

**999: Completion and Preparation for a New Chapter**

When you see 999, it's a message that a chapter in your life is ending. This number often appears during times of transition, signalling that it's time to release what has fulfilled its purpose. Seeing 999 invites you to embrace the end of this cycle with gratitude, as it makes way for new beginnings and experiences aligned with your spiritual growth.

**000: Oneness and Connection with the Divine**

The number 000 represents the infinite and reminds you of your oneness with the universe. This number often appears when you are in a moment of spiritual connection, letting you know that you are held in divine love. 000 is a reminder that you are never separate from the divine source, even in moments of doubt or fear. It's a call to trust the unity and interconnectedness of all things.

## *Discovering Your Sacred Number: A Path to Self-Awareness*

Uncovering your "life path number" can illuminate your spiritual mission and deepen your understanding of your unique place within the cosmic plan. This sacred number acts as a beacon, guiding you toward greater self-awareness and spiritual alignment.

The Language of Light calls us to look beyond spoken words and into the resonance of existence itself. When we embrace this divine form of communication, we find healing, wisdom and an abiding sense of universal love that nurtures and sustains us. In its light, we awaken to the truth that we are held, supported and infinitely cherished by forces beyond our imagination.

## *How to Embrace Angel Numbers in Daily Life*

Noticing angel numbers is just the first step. Embracing their messages fully allows us to open ourselves to the guidance and support the universe provides. Here's how to work with

**Example Calculation:**

- Birth date: July 15 (07/15)

  07 = 7

  15 = 1 + 5 = 6

  Total for birth date: 7 + 6 = 13 → 1 + 3 = 4

- Current year: 2024
  $2 + 0 + 2 + 4 = 8$

- Add the two results:
  4 (birth date) + 8 (current year) = 12 → 1 + 2 = 3

## *Meaning of the Personal Year Number:*

If your result is 3, your year is one of creativity, growth and self-expression. The energy of the number 3 calls you to tap into your inner creativity and express your truth without fear.

It is a year that encourages social connection, joy and sharing your talents with the world. You may find inspiration in new projects, artistic pursuits, or collaborative efforts that highlight your ability to communicate and inspire those around you.

Embracing the energy of your personal year number can guide your choices, reaffirm your intentions and help you navigate life with greater awareness and purpose. It reminds you that the universe is not a passive backdrop but an active participant in your spiritual journey, supporting you with love and wisdom through every cycle.

## *Calculating Your Life Path Number*

Your life path number, derived from your birth date provides insight into your personality and life's calling. Here's how to find it to deepen your spiritual awareness simple yet profound.

**Finding your life path number**

- Add Your Birth Month and Day

  Write down the month and day of your birth, simplifying each to a single digit if necessary.

- Add the Digits of the Current Year

  Reduce the year's digits to a single digit by summing them.

- Combine the Results

  Add the birth date sum to the year sum, reducing to a single digit if needed.

- Write Down Your Complete Birth Date

  For example, July 15, 1990, as 07/15/1990.

- Reduce Each Part of Your Birth Date to a Single Digit

  Month: 07 becomes 7.

  Day: 15 reduces to 1 + 5 = 6.

  Year: 1990 adds up to 1 + 9 + 9 + 0 = 19,
  which reduces to 1 + 9 = 10 and further to 1 + 0 = 1.

- Add the Reduced Numbers Together

  Add the month, day, and year totals: 7 + 6 + 1 = 14,

  which reduces to 1 + 4 = 5.

## *Understanding the Meaning of Single-Digit Numbers*

Each number carries unique vibrations, bet you become intrigued and gain more insight into frequency and geometry as you read.

**One – The Leader**

Embodies independence, initiative and ambition. Symbolizes new beginnings and inspires confidence and courage.

**Two – The Peacemaker**

Represents balance, harmony and partnership. Emphasizes relationships and working together to create unity.

**Three – The Creative Spirit**

Reflects joy, creativity and expression. Resonates with those who inspire through art and communication.

**Four – The Builder**

Stands for practicality, stability and hard work. Encourages discipline and a strong foundation.

**Five – The Adventurer**

Symbolises freedom, adaptability and exploration. Drawn to travel and embracing the unknown.

**Six – The Caregiver**

Focuses on love, nurturing and responsibility. Associated with family and selfless service.

**Seven – The Seeker**

Embodies spirituality and introspection. Seeks deeper truths and wisdom beyond the material world.

**Eight – The Achiever**

Reflects power, success and abundance. Excels in leadership and tangible impact.

**Nine – The Humanitarian**

Stands for compassion and generosity. Aims to uplift and serve humanity.

## *Special Significance of Master Numbers*

- **Eleven – The Intuitive Leader**
  Carries spiritual insight and the ability to inspire others.

- **Twenty-Two – The Master Builder**
  Combines practicality with vision, turning dreams into reality.

- **Thirty-Three – The Compassionate Teacher**
  Represents unconditional love and service to humanity.

## *Embracing Your Life Path Number*

Each number reveals strengths, challenges and lessons:

- **The Leader**: Inspires confidence and independence.
- **The Peacemaker**: Brings harmony and nurtures relationships.
- **The Creative Spirit**: Inspires through artistic expression.
- **The Builder**: Reliable and dedicated to growth.
- **The Adventurer**: Embraces change and exploration.
- **The Caregiver**: Radiates warmth and supports others.
- **The Seeker**: Guides others with introspective wisdom.
- **The Achiever**: Demonstrates ambition and success.
- **The Humanitarian**: Serves with empathy and generosity.
- **The Intuitive Leader**: Leads with spiritual awareness.
- **The Master Builder**: Blends practicality and vision.
- **The Compassionate Teacher**: Heals and uplifts others.

## *Your Personal Year Number*

Understanding your personal year number provides invaluable guidance, particularly when navigating significant personal goals or crossroads in your current year. While your sacred number reveals overarching patterns in your life's purpose, your personal year number highlights the unique themes, opportunities and challenges of this specific time. It serves as a compass, helping you focus your energy on what matters most right now. By attuning to this number, you can align with the spiritual rhythm of the year, gain clarity on pivotal decisions and ensure your choices support both your immediate aspirations and your long-term growth

To determine your personal year number, follow these steps:

**How to Calculate**

- **Add Your Birth Month and Day**

  Write down the month and day of your birth and reduce them to a single digit if necessary.

- **Add the Digits of the Current Year**

  Reduce the digits of the current year to a single digit by adding them together.

- **Combine the Results**

  Add the sum of your birth month and day to the single digit sum of the current year. Reduce the total to a single digit if needed.

  **Example**: Birth date: July 15 (07/15) 07 = 7  15 = 1 + 5 = 6

  Total for birth date: 7 + 6 = 13 → 1 + 3 = 4

  Current year: 2024  2 + 0 + 2 + 4 = 8

  Add the two results: 4 (birth date) + 8 (current year) = 12 → 1 + 2 = 3

  **Result**: Your personal year number is 3, indicating themes of creativity, growth and self-expression for the year.

## *The Spiritual Significance of Three*

In many spiritual traditions, the number three holds profound symbolism. It is often seen as representing completeness, balance and divine harmony. Examples include the Christian Holy Trinity (Father,

Son and Holy Spirit), the three Gunas in Hinduism (sattva, rajas and tamas) and the three pillars in Kabbalistic mysticism. Across various cultures, the concept of three represents a unity of body, mind and spirit, symbolising the fusion of personal will with divine intention. This triadic structure creates a powerful foundation for focusing spiritual energy.

## *How the Law of Three Amplifies Intention*

Throughout existence, sacred patterns reveal themselves not only in geometry and creation but also in the way energy flows and manifests. The *Law of Three* is one such principle, a universal force that amplifies intention, mirroring the divine balance found in the trinity of mind, body and spirit; past, present and future; birth, life and death the cycle of life. It is encoded in spiritual traditions, sacred architecture, and even the fundamental structures of the universe.

Repetition of an affirmation or question three times enhances its vibrational strength, grounding the intention more fully in both the conscious and subconscious mind. The first repetition plants the seed in waking awareness, allowing the thought to take form. The second repetition deepens it, weaving it into the subconscious where transformation begins. The third repetition acts as a bridge, carrying the intention beyond words into spiritual resonance, where it aligns with the unseen forces of creation.

This triadic rhythm echoes through ancient wisdom, reinforcing the idea that all energy sent forth in three's gains momentum, magnifying its reach.

For example, when seeking clarity, repeating a question such as, *"Is this path aligned with my highest good?"* activates different layers of perception. The first time, it is heard by the conscious mind, sparking awareness. The second time, it penetrates the subconscious, where deeper wisdom resides. The third time, it becomes more than a question it becomes a frequency, a vibration that harmonises with the universe, sending a clear signal to spiritual messenger, guides, the higher intelligence and the divine source of love God.

Mena, my Guardian Angel, once reminded me: *"Everything spoken with clarity and rhythm finds its way back to you."* This is the essence of the *Law of Three* a cosmic amplifier, turning whispers of intention into echoes across the infinite.

By embracing this sacred rhythm, we align ourselves with the natural order of the universe, strengthening the connection between thought, manifestation and divine guidance. In doing so, we do not merely *speak* our desires we *breathe* them into existence.

## *Practical Application of The Law of Three*

Here are some ways to incorporate this practice into daily life for deeper spiritual insights and clarity:

**Setting Intentions for Clarity:**

Begin each day by stating your intentions or desired outcomes three times aloud. For example, saying, "Today, I invite clarity and peace into my life" three times reinforces this intention and aligns your energy with these qualities, setting the tone for your day.

**Affirmations for Manifestation:**

When focusing on affirmations, repeat them three times with focused attention on each repetition. By doing this, you can feel the affirmation's energy resonate through your body, mind and spirit. For example: "I am worthy of love, abundance and joy." Saying it three times gives it a stronger foundation, affirming this belief at all levels of your being.

**Seeking Guidance through Questions:**

When unsure about a decision, try asking a question three times to invite clearer answers. For instance, if faced with a choice, repeat "Is this the right path for my growth?" three times slowly. Allow yourself to pause and listen after each repetition, noticing any thoughts, feelings or intuitive nudges that arise. The final repetition often yields the most profound insight. This process eliminates the wrong answers which may come from ego or negative mindset.

**Magnifying Prayer or Meditation:**

In meditation, use the Law of Three to enhance prayer or affirmations for spiritual protection, healing, or guidance. Repeating phrases such as "I am surrounded by light and love" three times can elevate your meditation, strengthening your energetic field and inviting a protective or healing presence.

**Recognising Divine Responses through Synchronicities**

When using the Law of Three, pay attention to synchronicities or intuitive signs that follow. Often, divine responses manifest as subtle coincidences, repeated symbols, or sudden moments of clarity. For example, after asking for guidance on a decision, you might notice a song lyric, a number sequence, or an unexpected conversation that aligns with your question.

These synchronicities serve as confirmations, letting you know that your intention was received and that you are supported by divine energies. Using consistently can help build trust in your inner guidance and spiritual connection.

Each time you experience a direct response, whether through intuition or synchronicity, your confidence and trust in the process grows. Over time, this practice strengthens your awareness of subtle messages from your Guardian Angels or higher self, nurturing a deeper sense of partnership with the divine.

**The Law of Three: Magnifying Intention through Repetition**

When we seek answers to life's meaningful questions like "Is this the right path for my growth?" our first response often arises from the part of us most focused on self-preservation and comfort.

This is the voice of the ego which in its simplest form is not a source of vanity but a well-meaning guardian of our comfort zone. It wants to keep us safe to help us avoid risk or uncertainty, but it can also hold us back from discovering the greater paths awaiting us. When we truly want guidance that goes beyond our immediate needs and desires the Law of Three can help us connect with a higher more loving source of wisdom.

## *How Ego Influences Our Initial Answers*

The ego's voice often reflects our anxieties our doubts or our need for external approval giving us answers that may be comforting but not necessarily aligned with our deepest growth. Here's how it can shape our first responses:

- Fear of the Unknown: The ego naturally avoids change offering safe but limited solutions that keep us within familiar bounds.
- Ingrained Beliefs: It may pull from past experiences or societal conditioning pushing us toward answers that don't honour our true selves.
- Desire for Approval: Often the ego wants us to choose paths that others will understand or praise even if they don't feel right in our hearts.

So, when we ask a question once especially a question with emotional weight the response might be shaped by fears or desires that reflect our ego's protective but often limiting nature.

## *Inviting Deeper Higher Guidance with the Law of Three*

Repeating a question three times helps create space for the true answer to emerge. With each repetition we quiet the mind releasing attachment to the ego's immediate response and inviting a more profound spiritually guided answer.

1. **First Repetition – honouring Our First Thoughts:**
   The first time we ask the question we're allowing our mind's natural concerns to come forward. This initial response often reflects our conditioned thoughts or insecurities, important to acknowledge but not necessarily aligned with our highest good. This first step is essential as it allows us to recognise and honour our fears without letting them control us.

2. **Second Repetition – Listening with Openness:**
   The second time we ask we move beyond those first layers of worry and defence. Here we can pause and begin to listen with an open-heart creating space for intuition. Often, we'll feel subtle shifts a sense of calm a release of tension or even a glimmer of curiosity or hope. This repetition invites us to consider the question beyond just what feels "safe" and to gently open to what feels "true."

3. **Third Repetition – Opening to Divine Guidance:**
   The third repetition we're inviting an answer from a higher more compassionate place within ourselves. In this moment the question becomes more than words; it becomes a prayer a call for divine insight that's free of ego's fears and doubts. The answer we receive now often carries a sense of peace reassurance or knowing that is unmistakably different.

Repeating a question or affirmation three times strengthens its energy. This practice invites clarity and deeper insight from your higher self, Guardian Angel. The Law of Three states that repeating a question or affirmation three times amplifies its power, strengthening the bridge between our awareness and divine response. For example, asking "Is this choice aligned with my highest good?" three times invites a clearer response from our Guardian Angels, often felt as intuition or seen in synchronicities.

This repetition builds trust and awareness of subtle signs, such as feelings of peace or timely conversations. It strengthens the relationship with our Guardian Angels and solidifies the trust in their guidance at the end of the day, you can apply the Law of Three to reflect on your experiences. Repeating questions like "What did I learn today?" or "How did I align with my purpose today?" three times helps you process the day's events on a deeper level. The repetition allows insights to emerge from within, offering new perspectives that may not be apparent at first. Building Trust in Your Spiritual Connection

## *Final Thought: honouring the Sacred Power of Three*

The Law of Three reminds us that the divine is accessible and actively responds to our intentions when approached with sincerity and focus. By fostering this powerful technique, we invite clarity to reinforce our purpose and open ourselves to trust our Guardian Angels divine support, which guides our journey with grace and wisdom. Through repetition we strengthen our intentions more securely, into our daily life allowing the creator to respond with loving guidance.

## *Nurturing Your Connection to Your Sacred Number*

Embrace your sacred number's qualities with self-love, gratitude and a sense of wonder. Through meditative practices, open your heart to your Guardian Angel's guidance, allowing their presence to align you with your soul's truth.

Engaging with sacred symbols and divine energies strengthens your connection to higher realms, nurturing your spirit and contributing to the collective compassion and healing of humanity. Practices such as meditation and reflection help integrate this divine connection into your daily life, offering continuous support and reassurance from the universe.

Sacred geometry and angel numbers serve as profound bridges between the seen and unseen, drawing us closer to the higher energies of the cosmos. When recognising, honouring and meditating on these symbols, we access a universal language that transcends words.

This language reminds us of the ever-present love and guidance of our Guardian Angels, who watch over us with infinite patience and care. These spiritual sacred practices assure us that we are never truly alone and that divine wisdom flows within us, one with God, one with the Earth, one with the Universe.

In moments of quiet reflection or meditation, allow yourself to tune into these sacred messages from spirit. Feel the unwavering support of your Guardian Angel trust in their gentle guidance and embrace the wisdom that reconnects you with your inner knowing.

It is my heartfelt hope that those who read these words will open themselves to the unconditional love offered to humanity, aiding both the ascension of planet Earth Gaia and the collective evolution of humanity.

*Sacred Geometry the flower of life*

CHAPTER 4

# Spiritual Self-Healing with Support from Your Guardian Angel

Have you ever felt a quiet ache deep within your heart, a longing for something you cannot fully name? It feels like a flicker of light buried beneath the surface, waiting for you to notice it. Or it feels like a soft whisper an inner knowing calling you to reconnect with something sacred within yourself. This is the intuitive healer within you, a divine spark that has always been there, patiently waiting to be rediscovered.

This spiritual presence does not demand your attention, nor does it push you to act. It simply waits with infinite love and compassion, inviting you to return to yourself. Healing is not about fixing something broken. It is about remembering the wholeness that has always been there, even in your most challenging moments. It is about honouring every part of your journey the joys, the struggles the spaces in between and finding the courage to soften where life has left you feeling hard or guarded.

Healing is also about trust. It is trusting in your capacity to heal and trusting in the support that surrounds you. This sacred process is not one you must navigate alone. You are deeply supported by a presence that knows your heart, your struggles and your joys. Your Guardian Angel walks beside you, not to judge or direct, but to guide and love you with unwavering compassion.

Your Guardian Angel is a bridge between your human experience and the divine realms. Through them you can access not only their love but also the infinite wisdom of the Archangels the divine kingdom of light and even your higher self. They are your closest ally, gently inviting you to embrace your divine essence and rediscover the love and light that have always been within you

## *The Practice of Connecting with Your Guardian Angel*

As with all new concepts, building a connection with your Guardian Angel begins with gentle, intentional practice. You do not need elaborate rituals or perfect words.

A simple moment of stillness where you open your heart and invite their presence into your life is enough. Over time, this connection will grow becoming a source of comfort guidance and transformation.

Close your eyes and imagine your Guardian Angel as a soft, radiant light surrounding you. This light is warm and steady, a reminder that you are held in love. You do not need to see or hear anything specific. Simply allow yourself to feel supported. Trust that your Guardian Angel is there, gently encouraging you to explore this sacred relationship at your own pace.

Your Guardian Angel will never push or impose. They will only guide you with love, helping you reconnect with the deeper truths of your soul. Through this connection, you may also begin to feel the presence of the Archangels, beings of divine light who carry specific frequencies of healing, protection and wisdom.

## *Michelle W's Story: A Healing Light*

Michelle W's journey with her Guardian Angel and personal team of spirit guides, began during a time of deep emotional pain she is an extremely sensitive empathic soul. On the surface, her life seemed fine always having an interest in all esoteric. She had a stable career and a loving family, but inside, she felt disconnected and heavy, burdened with a sense of emptiness she could not explain. At the suggestion of a friend, she attended a group meditation focused on angelic healing, though she entered the room with scepticism.

As the session began, Michelle struggled to relax. Her mind raced with doubts. She thought, "This won't work. Nothing will change." as the meditation deepened, something shifted. She felt a warmth surrounding her, like sunlight breaking through clouds. A soft melody filled the air and for the first time in years, her heart felt light.

Then, she heard a voice, not with her ears but within her soul. "You are not alone. You are loved.

You are whole." and gave her a name, tears streamed down her face as she realised, she was in the presence of her Guardian Angel, a being of pure love who had been walking beside her all along.

After that night, Michelle began a daily practice of connecting with her Guardian Angel. She would sit quietly each morning, close her eyes and simply say, "I invite you into my heart. Thank you for walking this journey with me." Over time, she felt a profound sense of peace and trust return to her life. Her burdens lightened and she began to see herself through the eyes of love.

Michelle's story is a reminder that healing does not happen all at once. It is a journey of small, meaningful steps, each one bringing you closer to the love that has always been within you.

## *A Visit from the Divine – The Stranger in the Sunlight*

A lady came to my clinic with a story that moved me to tears a sacred encounter she would carry with her for life.

She had been walking with her husband and their two young babies one sunny afternoon, enjoying a rare moment of peace after the birth of their second child. She had felt tired, but attributed it to the demands of motherhood, the sleepless nights and the emotional recovery that often follows a difficult birth.

As they strolled through the park, a complete stranger approached them. He was calm, radiant and held a gentle presence that immediately caught their attention.

"My dear one," he said softly, looking directly at her with eyes full of compassion, "you must go to the doctor. You are not well."

Startled, they paused. Her husband, sensing something unusual about the man not threatening, but deeply knowing invited him to speak more. Strangely, this stranger returned home with them. It was completely out of character, yet somehow, it felt divinely orchestrated.

The moment he stepped into their living room, things began to shift. The babies, usually restless, climbed into his lap and sat quietly. Their cat, typically aloof with visitors, curled up peacefully at his feet. The atmosphere changed. It felt as if time itself had paused.

The man turned to her and spoke with immense love and clarity.

"You have cancer. It is severe. You need to have your womb and ovaries removed urgently.

Listen, you are a good and kind person. You have so much to offer this world. You will face three severe struggles in your life but you will overcome them. You are here to be a channel of divine light."

Then he was gone.

His words proved heartbreakingly true. She was soon diagnosed with advanced cancer and underwent immediate surgery to save her life. She not only survived, but later faced two more trials that would test her spirit.

Years after her recovery, she fell gravely ill with pneumonia. Her family were told she had only three days to recover. She was on life support for three weeks. And yet she returned. She lived.

Not long after, she lost her beloved husband. It was a devastating loss. She carried on, not only surviving but continuing to serve her community with love and dedication. She became a nurse and carer, working tirelessly to support others right up until the time of the coronavirus pandemic.

It was during that time, hospitalised once again, that she was visited by an angel. She described a presence at her bedside that radiated light, warmth and peace. She knew in her heart that it was Divine. It was reassurance. It was pure love. All is well.

Now a grandmother, she continues to shine her light quietly, humbly and faithfully. The stranger in the sunlight never returned. His words, his truth and his love remain with her, always.

## *Reflection*

There are moments in life when the veil between the seen and unseen becomes thin when a word, a glance, or the appearance of a stranger can shift the course of our destiny. This heart-warming story reminds us, that we are never truly alone. Divine beings walk beside us, often unnoticed, guiding us with love and unwavering wisdom.

Take a moment now to reflect: Have you ever received a message that felt divinely timed? A warning, a blessing, a knowing that arrived when you needed it most? Breathe deeply, place your hand on your heart and ask your Guardian Angel to bring forth any memories or feelings that are ready to be healed or understood. Trust what rises. You and your loved ones are being held, guided and deeply loved always. Write them in your journal for reflection give thanks.

## *RW's Story: Following the Call*

RW is a dedicated medical professional who had spent years working long hours in a chaotic emergency ward. Though she loved helping people, she felt a quiet, persistent emptiness. She often wondered, "Is this all there is?"

During a clairvoyant reading, RW's Guardian Angel appeared vividly. She spoke with clarity and love, saying, "You are walking a noble path, but this is not where your soul is meant to stay. There is a greater calling waiting for you." The message struck a chord, awakening a dream RW had long buried, to bring healing to underserved communities around the world.

At first, the idea felt impossible. How could she leave her stable job? How could she uproot her life? Her Guardian Angel continued to guide her gently. One evening, she felt a strong feeling to check her email. There in her spam folder was a job posting for a medical position in a small village in Rwanda. RW's heart knew this was no coincidence.

With her Guardian Angel's guidance and the support of Archangels Michael and Gabriel, RW took the leap.

Today, she works in that village, bringing care and compassion to people who would otherwise go without. Her life is filled with purpose and joy and she often reflects on how her Guardian Angel's loving guidance led her to her soul's true calling.

## *Daniel's Story: A Quiet Miracle*

When Danial first came to angelic meditation he was desperately searching for answers. After losing his father suddenly, Daniel was consumed by grief and anxiety. He felt untethered, unable to move forward and tried to communicate through clairvoyants to no avail

One night, in desperation, he whispered, "If I have a Guardian Angel, please help me. I don't know what to do." That night, Daniel had a vivid dream. He stood by a river, bathed in golden light. Beside him was his father, who smiled warmly and another radiant figure whose presence filled Daniel with peace. Though the figure did not speak, Daniel felt a deep sense of comfort and love.

When he woke, Daniel did not feel all his pain disappear, but he felt supported. Encouraged by the dream, he began journaling and inviting his Guardian Angel into his daily life. Slowly, he began to feel lighter, his anxiety easing, his heart accepting and softening. Danial is now at peace a kind caring counsellor filling his life with purpose and contentment. Daniel's story shows how even the smallest act of trust can open the door to profound healing.

## *The Archangels: Divine Companions in Healing*

Through your connection with your Guardian Angel, you may feel drawn to invite the Archangels into your healing journey. Each Archangel carries a unique energy, offering specific gifts to support your growth and healing.

These divine beings, with their radiant presence, work harmoniously with your Guardian Angel to uplift, guide and empower you on your spiritual path:

- Archangel Raphael: Known as the divine healer, Raphael's emerald, green light brings soothing energy that addresses both physical and emotional wounds. Imagine this light surrounding you, gently dissolving tension and filling every part of you with a sense of renewal and vitality. Raphael's presence reminds you that healing is a natural process, one that flows effortlessly when love and self-compassion are welcomed.
- Archangel Michael: The protector and warrior of light, Michael's golden energy offers courage and strength when fear clouds your path. Picture him standing beside you, his sword of light cutting through doubts and negativity. With his shield raised, Michael assures you that you are safe and supported, giving you the confidence to face life's challenges with grace and resilience.
- Archangel Gabriel: The divine messenger, Gabriel's soft white light nurtures emotional healing and clarity of communication. When you feel overwhelmed or struggle to express your truth, invite Gabriel's presence into your heart. Imagine their light radiating around your throat and heart centres, helping

your words flow with ease and your emotions feel understood. Gabriel's guidance inspires creativity and brings a sense of hope.

- ❖ Archangel Metatron: Known as the keeper of sacred geometry and the scribe of the Akashic Records, Metatron's energy helps align you with your higher purpose. His radiant geometric light brings balance and clarity, empowering you to embrace your spiritual potential. Feel his energy surrounding you like a golden grid, gently harmonising your thoughts, emotions and intentions with the divine order of the universe.

Alongside these Archangels, you may also be intuitively guided to connect with Ascended Masters, enlightened beings who have transcended earthly limitations and now offer their wisdom and compassion to humanity. One such being is Master Djwal Khul, also known as "The Tibetan Monk."

## *A Journey of Light: Connecting with Master Djwal Khul and the Wisdom of Alice Bailey*

The books from Alice Bailey truly, is incredible she was humbled to be chosen by Djwal Khul to inform humanity of becoming light. When I first held her book in my hands, I felt an inexplicable pull, as if an unseen force had guided me to this sacred wisdom.

The words resonated deep within me, stirring something ancient in my soul. Alice Bailey completed trusted and accepted the messages from Master Djwal Khul to carry this light into the world, while reading her book. It felt both an honour and a responsibility that left me breathless with awe.

The teachings within these works are fundamental to spiritual practice. My personal story began when I first came across Alice Bailey's writings while training in spiritual healing. Guided by curiosity and with my Guardian Angel, Mena, I purchased her full collection. Whenever I encountered a passage

I struggled to understand, Mena would come to my aid, gently illuminating the meaning within my heart.

One evening, after immersing myself in *The Seven Rays*, I drifted into an uncharacteristically deep meditation. My body felt weightless, as if dissolving into pure energy. Then, I sensed a familiar presence, Mena, my beloved Guardian Angel. Gently, she guided me beyond the veil of the physical world.

Suddenly, I was in a luminous ashram, bathed in golden light. Around me sat scholars, radiant with wisdom, their eyes reflecting the depth of their souls.

At the front, Djwal Khul stood, his gaze steady yet kind, his presence like an eternal flame of truth. Alice Bailey sat among them, her expression serene. When our eyes met, she simply nodded, no words were needed. In that moment, I felt a profound knowing: I was exactly where I was meant to be. A wave of peace and love swept over me, settling deep within my soul, as if the universe itself had whispered, *Welcome home.* Bailey's works have since become one of my most recommended readings for my students.

Master Djwal Khul, also known as the Tibetan Monk, holds a revered place as a wise and compassionate guide. His influence became widely known through Alice Bailey's books, which remain foundational texts in esoteric philosophy. Between 1919 and 1949, Bailey wrote a series of works that she described as being dictated telepathically by Djwal Khul. These teachings explore profound spiritual concepts, including the nature of the soul, the process of spiritual evolution and humanity's role in the greater cosmic plan.

They emphasise personal transformation, service to humanity and alignment with divine will as pathways to enlightenment.

Djwal Khul's connection to Alice Bailey brought forward some of the most influential ideas in modern esotericism, including the Seven Rays of Energy, the Science of the Soul and the concept of spiritual hierarchy, a structure in which enlightened beings, including Ascended Masters, work together to guide humanity's evolution.

Djwal Khul taught that the soul is the bridge between the physical self and the divine essence. Healing and spiritual growth occur when we align with our soul's purpose, integrating its wisdom into our everyday lives.

The soul's journey is one of evolution, moving through cycles of growth, challenge and eventual liberation.

One of his most profound contributions was the teaching of the Seven Rays, seven distinct energies or forces that influence all of creation. Each person is said to be aligned with a specific ray that shapes their personality, soul and life purpose.

Understanding your ray can bring insight into your spiritual path and how you can best serve the world.

## *The Seven Rays are:*

Ray 1: Will and Power

Ray 2: Love and Wisdom

Ray 3: Active Intelligence

Ray 4: Harmony Through Conflict

Ray 5: Concrete Knowledge and Science

Ray 6: Devotion and Idealism

Ray 7: Ceremonial Order and Magic

When you connect with your Guardian Angel and the Ascended Masters, you can gain clarity on how these energies influence your life and how to harmonise them for healing and spiritual growth.

Djwal Khul emphasised the importance of service as a path to enlightenment. He taught that healing oneself is inseparable from serving others. When you heal, you not only align with your higher self but also contribute to the healing of the collective. This concept echoes through his writings as an invitation to view personal growth to uplift humanity.

A cornerstone of Djwal Khul's teachings is the practice of meditation as a tool for connecting with the soul, the higher self and the divine. He encouraged meditative techniques that focus on aligning the personality with the soul and cultivating clarity, balance and inner peace.

To connect with Master Djwal Khul, begin with a moment of stillness. Close your eyes and take a slow, deep breath. Feel the air filling your lungs, the gentle rhythm of life flowing through you. Now, imagine yourself standing at the entrance of a sacred temple, high in the mountains, where the air is crisp and filled with the scent of sandalwood and incense. The golden light of dawn spills through ancient archways, illuminating the worn stone beneath your feet.

As you step inside, a quiet stillness surrounds you, embracing you like an old friend. There, in the heart of the temple, sits Master Djwal Khul. His presence is steady, like the mountain itself, radiating wisdom, patience and infinite love. He lifts his gaze to meet yours and, in that instant, you feel seen, understood and profoundly held in the embrace of divine wisdom.

You whisper:

*"Master Djwal Khul, I humbly invite your presence into my heart and life. Guide me with your wisdom and love. Help me align with my soul's purpose and bring healing and light into my journey. May I serve with compassion and clarity, contributing to the greater good."*

Feel his energy surrounding you, a gentle, warm current, as if the universe itself were exhaling peace into your very being. Trust in this moment. You are exactly where you are meant to be.

Together, your Guardian Angel, the Archangels and Ascended Masters such as Djwal Khul form a divine network of love, guidance and wisdom. Each being offers their unique energy to support your healing, spiritual growth and alignment with your highest self.

Close your eyes and imagine this celestial team surrounding you in a circle of light. Your Guardian Angel stands closest to you, their presence familiar and comforting. The Archangels stand just beyond, each radiating their unique colours, green for Raphael, gold for Michael, white for Gabriel and golden geometric patterns for Metatron. Beyond them, Djwal Khul and other Ascended Masters watch over you, their love steady and unconditional.

Feel their combined energy pouring into you, filling you with a profound sense of peace, strength and clarity. Trust that you are never alone. This divine support is always available to you, waiting for you to invite it into your heart. You are deeply loved, infinitely supported and guided every step of the way.

You are not alone on this journey. Your Guardian Angel walks with you, always ready to guide you, to hold space for your healing and to remind you of the light within you. Healing is not something to rush or force. It is an unfolding, a gentle process of rediscovering the wholeness and love that have always been yours.

Place your hand over your heart and breathe deeply. Feel the steady rhythm of your soul, a sacred reminder that you are loved, supported and connected to infinite divine light. Trust that your Guardian Angel is with you in every moment, guiding you home to yourself. You are deeply loved, infinitely supported, complete and whole. All is well.

*Guardian Angel*

CHAPTER 5

# The Art of Spiritual Journaling

Imagine the moment you pick up a pen, the cool weight of it in your hand, the smooth glide of its tip across a blank page. Now, think of this pen as more than just a tool; it is an extension of your higher mind, a bridge between worlds, a sacred key unlocking the wisdom of your soul.

Spiritual journaling is not simply writing. It is an act of deep listening. Each stroke of ink carries energy, intention, and messages waiting to be revealed. Words become a mirror, reflecting your inner world and allowing hidden truths to rise gently to the surface.

From the dawn of human history, great civilizations have understood writing to be a sacred act, a way to connect with spirit. Ancient cultures, from Egyptian scribes to Indian sages, from cave painters to Mesoamerican mystics, left behind symbols, texts, and carvings: living prayers encoded with divine wisdom.

## *Journaling as Sacred Conversation*

Journaling is more than a record of thoughts, it is a way of awakening your higher intelligence. It calms the mind, opens the heart, and invites divine guidance. It becomes a sacred conversation between your soul and the universe, a personal ritual that can heal, transform, and expand consciousness.

What's truly beautiful is that modern science now supports what ancient mystics have always known: the act of expressive writing and self-reflection can have profound effects on mental, emotional, and even physical well-being.

Numerous studies have shown that journaling can reduce symptoms of anxiety, depression, and stress. According to research in psychology and neuroscience, writing about our thoughts and feelings engages the brain's prefrontal cortex, the area responsible for regulation, reflection, and insight. When we write, especially with mindful intention, we're not just expressing we're rewiring.

Neural pathways linked to emotional healing begin to strengthen, and the brain shifts into a more balanced, regulated state.

Spiritual journaling also aligns with the practice of mindfulness, which is now widely recognised by mental health professionals as a powerful tool for improving emotional resilience and mental clarity. It brings us fully into the present moment, slowing down the mind and grounding us in our truth.

Your journal becomes your friend, your confidant the one who listens without judgment. When you feel lost, confused, or burdened by worry, your journal is there to receive your thoughts. With every word you write, you release what no longer serves you. You hand over your concerns, fears, and doubts to your Guardian Angel, trusting they will be carried away and transformed into light. In their place, you invite peace, clarity, and faith.

If a painful thought arises, respect it. Acknowledge it. Then gently explore how it feels to replace it with a positive affirmation.

Instead of writing, *"I am afraid,"* you might write, *"I am safe and guided."*

Instead of *"I feel lost,"* you affirm, *"I trust my path is unfolding perfectly."*

Every entry becomes an act of alchemy, shifting your energy from darkness to light. And sometimes, it's enough just to admit: *"Today feels heavy."* Accepting that is part of your healing. When you call to your Guardian Angel, your divine wisdom steps clearly into your mind, gently reassuring you: *All is well.*

Through this sacred practice, you begin to see how writing shapes your inner world, turning chaos into clarity, pain into wisdom, and fear into love.

## *A Personal Story of Healing*

I remember a time when I felt deeply anxious and didn't even know why. The uneasiness sat heavy in my chest, like an invisible weight pressing down. I decided to write, hoping the words would help me understand.

As I let my pen move freely, what poured onto the page surprised me. I wrote with deep frustration and anger toward a colleague, someone I believed was deliberately blocking my career.

I felt ignored, unappreciated, and unfairly held back. The words kept coming, raw and unfiltered. I was angry with her, but underneath it all, I was even more upset with my Guardian Angel and with God.

I felt abandoned. Unsupported. As if my prayers had gone unanswered. I wanted to speak my truth, to confront her, but fear held me back, fear of losing my job, making things worse, or falling into financial instability when I had responsibilities I couldn't walk away from.

I felt trapped. Trapped by circumstance. Trapped by life itself.

Days later, I returned to that page. The weight of my emotions hit me all over again. I hadn't realised how much pain I had been carrying. I sat with it, acknowledged it, and then closed my eyes. I asked my Guardian Angel for help. In my mind's eye, I imagined wrapping all those emotions my anger, frustration, and fear into a soft, pink, fluffy blanket. I handed them over with deep intention, trusting they would be held and transformed.

Something shifted. I felt lighter, as if the burden was no longer mine to carry. It didn't happen all at once, but over the days that followed, a sense of peace began to grow. Forgiveness settled not just for my colleague, but for myself.

I realised I had been blaming others, when in truth, I was the one holding myself back.

A little while later, everything looked different. My colleague wasn't holding me back no one was.

The only thing limiting me was my belief that I was powerless.

That clarity changed me. Journaling had given me the space to face my emotions honestly, to process them, and to invite divine energy into my healing. Writing didn't just uncover my pain it helped me release it.

## *The Divine and Scientific Energy of Writing*

Journaling quiets the mind and brings awareness to life's deeper journey. The act of writing engages both the logical and intuitive parts of the brain, creating harmony between thought and feeling, body and spirit.

Scientific research confirms what spiritual traditions have always taught: journaling lowers cortisol levels (the stress hormone), improves emotional regulation, and supports resilience. It's now used in therapy, coaching, and wellness practices around the world, helping people understand their inner world and gently transform it.

Just as sacred sound shapes vibration, written words shape emotion and experience.

## *Timeless Wisdom Through the Ages*

This practice isn't new it is eternal.

Long before paper and pen, people carved symbols into stone, clay, and temple walls. The ancient Egyptians believed writing was a divine gift. Scribes were not just record keepers but spiritual intermediaries, guided by Thoth, the god of wisdom and writing. Each symbol in Egyptian hieroglyphs held layers of meaning, acting as a bridge between human thought and cosmic truth. Their sacred texts, such as the *Book of the Dead,* contained guidance for the soul's journey, revealing that words had the power to shape reality, even in the afterlife.

Early humans painted symbols and images on cave walls. These were not simply drawings, but deep thought, acts of communion with spirit. Shamans believed that recording visions in sacred places called forth the guidance of spirit guides, ancestors and the wisdom of the natural world.

The Maya and Aztecs used writing to track cosmic cycles and divine messages. Their codices, made from sacred tree bark, contained celestial patterns and prophecies. The Maya believed that time itself was a cycle of spiritual lessons, recorded by scribes who were messengers of the gods.

In ancient India, writing was considered a way to capture sacred sound. The Vedas some of the world's oldest spiritual texts were first spoken aloud, then written on palm leaves. Each word was believed to carry vibrational energy that could shape reality itself.

## *The Creation of this Book.*

Years of heartfelt journaling became the roots of these chapters. My journals became my safe place, my sanctuary. Not every entry looked like neat lines of words. Sometimes, when I was overwhelmed or upset, especially during times when my dyslexia felt more intense, my entries were scribbles, diagrams, shapes and symbols. At times, my emotions were too big for words and that was okay. My journal held it all without judgment.

It was my emotional outlet, my refuge, my way to process the world when I couldn't always speak it out loud or write it down clearly. In those raw, unfiltered pages, I met the deepest parts of myself. I met my truth.

And slowly, through those scribbled moments of pain, deep thought, joy, and surrender, these words emerged. This book is not just a collection of teachings it's a living journey, born from the healing space of journaling. A space that anyone can access.

## *A Loving Invitation*

Let your journal be a loving witness to your journey. Let it hold your truth with gentleness. Let it be your place of transformation, where pain becomes prayer, and doubt becomes deep faith.

May your pen flow freely.

May your heart feel heard.

And may your soul know that it is always, always supported.

## *Your Turn: A Sacred Beginning*

I would to invite you to begin.

Open your journal see a blank page. Take a breath. Let your hand soften and draw a simple circle.

This is your starting point, no pressure, no right or wrong.

As you gaze into that circle, notice what begins to come to mind. A thought, a colour, a memory, a shape. Let it be free. Let it flow. This simple act becomes a doorway a sacred symbol of wholeness and possibility.

You may find that your higher mind begins to accept this new way of communicating. Intuitive words may emerge. Dreams may rise to the surface. Emotions may pour through in images or symbols rather than sentences. Allow them.

Let this moment be your first step in connecting with your soul through the art of spiritual journaling. Trust that whatever comes is enough. Trust that your Guardian Angel is near.

The circle is open.

Your sacred conversation has begun.

CHAPTER 6

# Ascension as a Path to Inner Peace – The Discovery of Awakening

## *Developing Inner Knowing*

Ascension is not about leaving this world behind; it is about rising within it, expanding into a state of profound awareness where you align with divine love, wisdom, and healing. It is a journey of returning home, to your authentic self, to your soul's wisdom, and to the ever present guidance of Spirit that flows through all things. It is not a path of striving or achieving; it is a path of remembering.

Remembering who truly are, remembering the boundless joy and love that has always surrounded you.

Many people think of ascension as an external process, a destination to reach. I believe true ascension is an inner transformation. It is not about moving higher, it is about going deeper. It is about dissolving illusions, releasing fear, and opening our heart to the divine flow of the universe. It is about stepping into a space where you accept, trust, not because you have seen the path ahead, but because you have felt its truth in your soul.

In the quiet spaces within, we rediscover the sacred connection that has never left us. Yet, in today's world, where artificial light replaces the soft glow of the moon and the hum of technology drowns out the sound of birdsong and the whisper of the wind, many have lost touch with this ancient knowing. We move too fast, burdened by endless tasks; our minds cluttered with distractions that pull us away from the simplicity of being. The world urges us to seek answers outside of ourselves, yet the deepest wisdom has always been within.

This connection strengthens not only through mindfulness and meditation, but through experiencing the world with all six senses and the seventh sense, the spiritual awareness that ties everything together.

Imagine or try ...

Walking barefoot on the earth feeling the cool damp grass under your feet and the warm light of the sun on your skin. The air is rich with the scent of pine and wildflowers mixing with the sweet earthy aroma of moss covered stones.

As you breathe deeply you taste the fresh morning air cool and clear tinged with the hint of dew. The sunlight filters through the trees casting soft shifting patterns of light and shadow while the gentle rustling of leaves and the distant call of birds create a melody that speaks to your soul.

In these moments you are not just in nature you are part of it and in that connection, you find Spirit.

Invite your Guardian Angel to walk with you, to create sacred spaces. Their guidance is never loud or forceful it is gentle and loving like a soft breeze on your face or the warmth that blooms unexpectedly in your heart.

As you tune into this presence you notice signs all around you, a feather resting on your path the sudden flight of a butterfly the feeling of calm wrapping around, the huge grin on your face just when you need it most. These are not coincidences they are reminders that you are deeply connected to the Divine that you are supported loved and guided.

## *The Lost Continent of Atlantis*

I remember the exact moment it all unfolded.

I was in Crete, Greece, sitting atop a majestic mountain, overlooking the calm, endless blue of the Aegean Sea. The warm sun bathed my skin, a golden embrace from the heavens, while a soft breeze carried the scent of salt and wildflowers. The vastness before me was breathtaking crystal clear turquoise waters stretching beyond the horizon, waves shimmering like liquid light.

In that stillness, something shifted.

A presence surrounded me, gentle, radiant, deeply familiar. Mena, my Guardian Angel, stood beside me, her energy like a warm embrace, a whisper of ancient knowing. She spoke without words, her voice flowing through my heart rather than my ears.

*"Let me show you something you have always known,"* she said.

And in an instant, the veil lifted.

Before my eyes, Atlantis rose from the depths, not as a lost ruin, but as a living, thriving reality. Towering crystalline structures sparkled in the sunlight, their surfaces reflecting the golden hues of dawn and dusk. The air quietly gently hummed with energy, filled with the music of unconditional love creation, the purest harmony of existence.

Atlantis isn't lost at all it lives within each and every one of us. It is not just a place of legend but a vibration, a state of being, a memory etched into the soul.

Through my channelled meditation in Chapter 10, I will take you there to a realm of unconditional love, where no pain, no fear, and no death exist. Here we live in harmony with ancient, prehistoric animals, walking alongside magnificent beings of every form majestic woolly mammoths, gentle sabre-toothed cats, and winged creatures that once graced the skies. Every living being radiates kindness and intelligence, connected through light, frequency, and love.

In Atlantis, higher intelligence flourishes, and beings exist in an elevated state of consciousness, vibrating at a higher frequency of pure light. Telepathy and clairvoyance are as natural as breathing thoughts flow effortlessly between hearts, and wisdom is shared instantly, beyond words. Every plant, every creature, every shimmering drop of water sings in harmony, offering its own unique frequency of love.

The people of Atlantis live in awe-inspiring cities, where highly advanced technology blends seamlessly with nature. Towering crystalline structures, powered by solar energy, rise into the sky, reflecting the colours of the heavens.

Fresh water flows endlessly, drawn from natural springs, purified by the very essence of the Earth. The entire infrastructure supports a world where humanity thrives free from burden, in balance with the universe.

Travel is effortless beings move by beams of light, flowing from place to place with the power of thought and intention. There is no rush, no struggle only the graceful unfolding of existence.

And through all of this, there is a deep, unwavering love and respect for the elders the keepers of wisdom, the storytellers of past and future. It was heartwarming to see a young boy guiding his grandfather to the sacred spring, their hands intertwined, their bond unbreakable. Here, age is not feared, but cherished a journey of infinite learning, where the soul only grows brighter with time.

And even now, you can still see glimpses of Atlantis, in the brilliance of a golden sunset, in the arching colours of a rainbow, in the way the sun's beams dance upon the earth. It reveals itself in the crystal clear turquoise oceans, the quiet majesty of sunrise, and the infinite depth of nature. Feel it in the gentle rustling of leaves, the warmth of the sun on your skin, the soft embrace of the wind.

You can see it in the eyes of animals full of ancient wisdom, trust, and love. You can feel it in the innocent laughter of children, in the radiant gaze of a newborn baby, where the purity of the soul shines through, untouched by time. These are not just fleeting moments of beauty; they are reminders of a world we are returning to, a vibration we are awakening within ourselves.

This world is not a dream it is already within us, waiting to be remembered. As we awaken, as we choose love, we bring Atlantis back to life.

Atlantis is waiting for you. Are you ready to return?

## *Nurturing a Daily Connection with Your Guardian Angel*

The purpose of writing this book is to encourage humanity to reconnect with their Guardian Angel who is a divine messenger of God. It does not require grand rituals or complicated practices. Their presence thrives in the simple heartfelt moments when you step away from the artificial and open yourself to the beauty of the natural world. Begin your morning with gratitude feeling the warmth of the sun on your face the cool morning air filling your lungs the soft touch of the earth beneath your feet.

As you breathe deeply invite their presence into your day letting each breath ground you in the present moment.

## *The Spiritual Connection of Loving-Kindness*

Discovering self-healing is an act of unconditional love, not only for yourself but for the divine spark that has always lived within you. It is a sacred journey, a homecoming of the soul, where body, mind, and spirit realign, fostering resilience, peace, and a deep remembrance of who you truly are.

When you take time to practice the seven steps outlined in my book, you are sending a message to your soul: *I am ready to awaken.* At first, this message is a whisper, a ripple in the still waters of your being. But as you continue, as you surrender to the practice, the whisper becomes a call, a song, a vibration that your soul recognises. And it listens.

As you hold your pendulum, let your hands grow still, your breath deepens, and trust that your Guardian Angel is nearby. Their presence is not a distant, unreachable force, it is beside you, within you, guiding your hands, steadying your heart, raising your vibration. Close your eyes. Feel the energy stir around you, gentle yet powerful, like a tide that carries you effortlessly toward the shores of higher consciousness.

Pause for a moment. Inhale deeply. Can you sense the quiet hum of life within you? This is your Divine light, ancient, infinite, unwavering. It has never left you. Trust it. Let it illuminate your path, raising your frequency, softening the barriers you have built, and radiating love beyond the limits of what you thought possible.

It is not something distant or something we must chase or earn. It is here all always, embedded in the core of our existence. It is in every breath we breath the gentleness of the wind that brushes against our skin, the rhythmic rise and fall of the ocean's tides, the first golden rays of dawn spilling across the horizon. Spirit moves through the laughter of a child, in the fragrance of jasmine blooming at night, in the hush of an ancient forest untouched by time. Every blade of grass, every drop of rain, every flickering star in the vast night sky carries the presence of the Divine.

And when we awaken to this truth, something within us shifts. We remember.

There is a sacred language beyond words, spoken in the quiet murmurs of the earth itself. Imagine walking barefoot on the cool, damp ground, the rich scent of pine and wildflowers filling the air. Feel the warmth of the sun resting gently on your skin, the freshness of the morning mist awakening your senses. Sunlight filters through the trees, casting golden patterns across the forest floor. The world breathes, and in its breath, you hear a song, a lullaby of creation, a whisper of love, a call to be still, to listen, to simply *be.*

In these moments, you are not just in nature. You *are* nature. You are not separate from the world around you; you are woven into it, a thread in the great tapestry of existence, moving in harmony with the unseen rhythm of the universe.

Close your eyes, invite your Guardian Angel to walk beside you, their presence is not loud not demanding, it is a soft, steady glow, a gentle current of love wrapping around your heart. When you open yourself to this. You notice recurring signs: a feather resting on your path, a red robin visiting, a butterfly landing delicately nearby, a persistent cat giving you unconditional love an unshakable sense of peace flooding through you when you're in a moment of stillness.

These are not coincidences. They are whispers from your Guardian Angel the Divine messenger from God offering quiet reminders that you are never alone.

Take a deep breath. Feel the earth beneath your feet, anchoring you. Feel the embrace of divine love surrounding you, reminding you that you are safe, that you are held, that you are infinitely supported.

Know this: you are already rising, not by force, but by surrender. You are ascending, not by grasping, but by allowing.

And in that surrender, in that allowing, you find your truest authentic self.

When you step outdoors let your senses awaken. For this is where divine love flows. Feel the rough texture of tree bark beneath your fingertips grounding you in the ancient wisdom of the earth Inhale the woody scent of pine the sweet aroma of flowers in bloom the earthy richness of the ground after a gentle rain. Taste the air fresh and cool carrying the faint hint of salt from the sea or the sweetness of wildflowers drifting on the breeze.

Watch as the sunlight dances through the leaves casting golden patterns on the ground Listen to the world coming alive the rustle of leaves in the wind the soft hum of bees the quiet trickle of water in a nearby stream. Even in stillness the world speaks and through its Spirit reaches out to you.

As you move through your day, pause often to reconnect. Notice the taste of your morning tea the coolness of a crisp winter air or the warmth of the sun on your skin, feel of the earth beneath your feet grounding, balancing your energy. These simple moments are invitations to remember that you are never alone. Your Guardian Angel walks beside you are offering gentle guidance and unwavering unconditional love.

Choosing to live this way, to truly live rather than merely exist, you open yourself to a life filled with love abundance joy peace and contentment.

The natural world becomes a mirror reflecting the beauty and divinity within you. Every sunrise is a new beginning every drop of rain a blessing every breeze a reminder that Spirit flows through all things including you.

This is the secret magical connection humanity needs now, more than ever a return to the heart of the earth to Spirit. Awakening your senses and stepping into the natural world you rediscover the divine presence that has always been with you guiding you to live fully love deeply and walk in harmony with all that is in nature all of creation.

Embarking on the path of self-healing is an act of profound self-love. It invites you to listen attentively to your most essential needs, uncovering the strength and resilience that have always been within you.

## *The Ancient Art of Tree Bathing and Hugging*

Long before the rush of modern life pulled us into its whirlwind, humanity lived in quiet harmony with the natural world. The ancient art of tree bathing and tree hugging is a beautiful return to that connection, a gentle, mindful practice that invites us to slow down, breathe deeply, and remember that we are part of something much greater than ourselves. It is not simply about being in nature but *communing* with it, feeling the pulse of life that runs through every tree, every leaf, every whisper of wind.

Tree bathing, known in some cultures as *shinrin-yoku*, is the act of immersing oneself in the presence of trees, allowing their energy and tranquillity to wash over you. It is more than just walking through the forest; it is about *being* with the trees, allowing your senses to fully open. You feel the roughness of the bark beneath your fingers, grounding you with its ancient strength. You breathe in the rich, earthy scent of the forest floor, mingling with the fresh, green aroma of leaves and the subtle sweetness of sap.

The sounds of rustling leaves, the distant calls of birds, and the gentle creak of branches in the breeze form a natural symphony that soothes the mind and quiets the heart.

Tree hugging, often misunderstood or dismissed in our hurried world, is a simple yet profound act of connection. When you wrap your arms around a tree, you are not just embracing wood and bark, you are embracing a living being that has stood the test of time, weathered storms, and soaked up the sun for decades, even centuries.

The tree welcomes you without judgment, offering its silent strength and steady presence. You may feel a subtle warmth radiating from its core or a calming stillness that seeps into your own heart. In that moment, you and the tree are no longer separate, you are connected through the invisible threads of life and spirit that bind all living things.

Science has only recently begun to catch up with what ancient cultures have always known: that trees and forests nature has the power to heal. Time spent among trees has been shown to reduce stress, lower blood pressure, and boost the immune system. Beyond the physical benefits, tree bathing and hugging nourish the soul. They remind us to slow down, to breathe, to listen. They teach us the art of presence and patience, showing us that life does not always need to be rushed or filled with noise.

In embracing the ancient art of tree bathing and hugging, we are not just finding peace within ourselves, we are honouring the sacred relationship between humanity and nature. We are remembering that we are not separate from the earth but deeply intertwined with it. Each tree holds the wisdom of the ages, and by connecting with them, we tap into that timeless knowledge.

So, the next time you find yourself near a tree, pause for a moment. Rest your hand against its trunk. Breathe in its scent. Listen to the quiet song it sings through its leaves. And when you are ready, wrap your arms around it. Feel its heartbeat. Let it remind you that you are supported, grounded, and deeply loved by the earth itself.

## *The Damson Tree That Spoke to Me*

Long before tree hugging was ever a 'thing' before anyone gave it a name. It would have been considered a strange thing to do.

My personal experience was quite different from others as I had already found my heart wrapped around a tree. As a child I adored the old damson tree that stood proudly in our garden Its gnarled branches, were my playground my fortress and my secret hiding spot. I would drape old sheets over its limbs to build shelters imagining them as castles or faraway forts.

As I grew braver, I climbed higher and higher feeling the rough bark beneath my fingers the wind brushing through my hair and the steady comforting strength of the tree holding me up.

It was not just a tree to me it was a friend a guardian, I believed it listened when I spoke, that it understood the quiet thoughts I never voiced to anyone else.

One day as I scrambled up the familiar branches something felt different, I paused halfway my hand resting on a limb that suddenly felt off. The tree spoke to me not with words like people use but with a deep knowing that resonated inside me. Stop climbing it seemed to whisper this branch is sick. I froze my heart thudding; I looked up and saw how that branch stretched out heavy and brittle hanging right over our large glass greenhouse.

I scrambled down my mind racing and later that day I saw my dad walking toward the damson tree with a saw in hand.

Panic welled up in me I ran to him breathless pleading, Dad waits! Let me talk to the tree first. He paused probably thinking his little girl had lost her marbles but to his credit, he set the saw down and gave me that patient look only a father can give. I wrapped my arms around the tree pressing my cheek against its rough bark tears spilling freely.

My heart felt heavy full of sorrow as if I was about to lose an old friend, then the tree spoke to me again soft and kind, I know it whispered It is time I am getting old and I am a danger now.

Tell your Dad not to cut me down completely, I will pull my life force away from the diseased branches and I will still bear fruit.

I wiped my tears heart pounding with a mix of sadness and hope, and I turned to tell my Dad.

I must have looked a sight, my face streaked with tears eyes wide and earnest. He listened quietly as I shared what the tree had told me. He did not laugh; He did not brush me off. Instead, he knelt looked me straight in the eyes and said I know why you love this tree pet. You know it is dangerous It would break my heart if you or one of your brothers or sisters got hurt from those dead branches. I will only cut off the ones that are sick believe and trust me.

Relief flooded through me; I threw my arms around him hugging him tight before dashing off to find my Mum. When I told her she pulled me close smoothing my hair and said with a soft smile. We will still get some lovely damsons and make our favourite jam just like always.

And we did! The tree kept its promise, even after Dad trimmed away the sick branches the damson tree continued to bloom offering its sweet dark fruit year after year It stood tall in the garden a little worn a little scarred but alive, still my friend still a part of our family.

Looking back, I realise now that the damson tree taught me more than just how to climb or how to listen. It showed me that everything living carries wisdom that the natural world speaks, if we are quite enough to hear. It taught me about unconditional love, loss acceptance and the beauty of letting go. Without giving up and perhaps most importantly it reminded me that even as we grow older like that beloved tree there is always life and purpose in the parts of us that remain.

## *The Little Acorn That Grew*

When my son was just four years old, he came home from nursery one day, his face lit with excitement, in his small hands he held a plastic cup filled with soil and a tiny acorn nestled inside.

With wide eyes he told me, Mummy one day this will grow into a gigantic oak tree taller than Daddy taller than our house, I smiled at his wonder and nodded agreeing with his grand vision. After he dashed off to play, I knelt by the little acorn cup speaking softly to the tiny oak within. My little boy has great expectations, I whispered enjoy this warm little border for now and when the time comes, I will move you to a greater space where you can stretch and grow tall and strong.

Years passed, the seasons turned, and the tiny acorn grew into a small sapling nestled happily in the border among my flowers One sunny afternoon while tending to the garden I noticed the young oak standing proudly its leaves rustling softly in the breeze. I felt her presence strong and clear and as I leaned closer, she spoke to me in that quiet way only nature can She asked if she could be moved to a larger space but gently told me to wait a little longer so she could pull her energy back from her roots I nodded respecting her wishes and left her to prepare

In the meantime, I wandered to the very bottom of my garden feeling the earth beneath my feet and letting the garden's energy guide me I asked where this little sapling should go, and the garden led me to the far right-hand corner. A calm certainty filled me as I dug a small hole in the rich earth blessing it with gratitude and intention for the life it would soon hold.

When I returned to the sapling, I knelt beside her asking softly if she was ready. She responded with a gentle yes and I carefully respect-fully loosened the soil around her roots lifting her with care I carried her to the corner of the garden cradling her as if she were a precious treasure and planted her in her new home. Nestled in the earth she seemed to settle immediately as though she had been waiting for this exact moment.

Years have passed since that day The little acorn grew into a mighty oak tree her branches reaching high into the sky her leaves dancing in the wind, she stands strong and proud abundant with acorns each season new saplings grow beneath her shade and I share them with others gifting pieces of her spirit to those who will nurture them in new places

I have photographed her journey over the years capturing the beauty of her growth and sharing it on my website www.healingtouch.uk.com.

Each image tells a story of patience trust and the quiet wisdom that nature offers if we choose to listen.

Though my son has never climbed the oak tree that grew from his tiny acorn I often wonder if one day his child will.

Perhaps his own little one will look up at the towering branches with the same awe and wonder that he once held in his heart and the cycle will continue as it always does with nature guiding us gently along the way.

This chapter offers an opportunity to explore practices that honour the interconnectedness of body, mind, and spirit.

## *The Sacred Journey of Natural Living and Self-Healing*

Long before tree hugging became a trend or naturopathy found its way into wellness circles, I instinctively lived a life deeply connected to nature and its rhythms. As a child, I found solace under the branches of our old damson tree, speaking to it as a friend and listening to its quiet wisdom. That early connection to the natural world has shaped my entire journey, guiding me toward a life of balance, mindfulness, and self-healing.

Living naturally and intuitively has always been my way of life. If I had to give it a name, it would be naturopathy. Being vegetarian and avoiding eggs is part of this journey. As a child, our family turned to home remedies instead of medication unless the illness was serious. We ate wholesome, naturally grown food, spent most of our time outdoors, and lived without worry. Life was simple, and its simplicity was healing.

## *The Foundations of Naturopathy and Holistic Healing*

True self-healing goes beyond addressing physical symptoms; it involves nurturing the entire person, body, mind, and spirit. This principle lies at the heart of naturopathy, an ancient practice based on the belief that the body possesses an inherent capacity for healing when balanced with nature. Hippocrates, known as the "Father of Medicine," famously stated, "The natural healing force within each of us is the greatest force in getting well," viewing the body as an integral part of the natural world, responsive to its rhythms and constantly connected to its surroundings.

Hippocrates' teachings remind us that we are micro-organisms within a greater macro-organism, part of Earth's ecosystem. Even in death, we return to the earth, continuing the cycle of life. This holistic view recognises that true well-being encompasses physical health, emotional states, relationships, and our spiritual connection with the divine.

While modern medicine increasingly acknowledges this interconnectedness, some healthcare systems, such as the UK's, often remain symptom-focused rather than person-centred. This approach overlooks the deeper truth that health and illness mirror our inner harmony or disharmony with life. Ancient wisdom teaches that genuine healing aligns the body, mind, and soul with the universe's greater rhythms. However, life's challenges, such as difficult relationships or personal imbalances, can trigger emotions of anger, frustration, and resentment.

## *Forgiveness as a Path to Healing*

From an esoteric viewpoint, the path to healing and forgiveness is powerful. Forgiveness transcends a simple decision; it is an act of surrender to a higher power. Releasing anger, hate, jealousy or frustration and entrusting these emotions to a power we believe, is greater than our own its Divine, when practiced daily, we create space for self-healing that surpasses human understanding. This surrender invites peace to replace pain and fosters compassion, loving kindness not only for us but for our ancestors and the greater collective.

Choosing forgiveness invites healing light into our lives and extends it to those who have wronged us.

The angelic realm supports this process; invoking love and light three times calls to divine beings to mend even the most fractured relationships. This practice bridges human limitations and heals emotional wounds that might otherwise remain unresolved especially those in spirit.

## *Holistic Healing Across Cultures*

Self-healing is a universal practice, rooted in the wisdom of diverse traditions from around the world. Each culture offers unique insights into nurturing the body, mind, and spirit, reminding us of the interconnectedness of all life.

**In Japan, the concept of *ikigai*.** translated as "reason for being", encourages individuals to align their passions, skills, and contributions to society. This purposeful approach to life has been linked to the longevity and vitality of communities such as Okinawa, often referred to as one of the world's "Blue Zones." Complementing this, Japanese practices like *shinrin-yoku* (forest bathing) emphasise reconnecting with nature for stress reduction and emotional balance.

**In India, *Ayurveda*,** a system of medicine dating back over 5,000 years, emphasises balance within the three doshas (vata, pitta, kapha) to achieve optimal health. This is achieved through personalised diets, herbal remedies, yoga, and meditation. The practice of yoga, with its eightfold path (*ashtanga*), fosters not only physical flexibility but also spiritual awakening, emphasising the union of body and mind.

**In China, *Traditional Chinese Medicine (TCM)*** offers a holistic approach to health, focusing on the balance of *yin* and *yang* and the flow of *qi* (life force) through meridians in the body. Techniques like acupuncture, tai chi, and herbal medicine aim to restore harmony and vitality.

**In Europe,** centuries-old herbalism remains a cornerstone of holistic health. Remedies like chamomile (for relaxation), St. John's wort (for mood enhancement), and elderberry (for immunity) have been passed down through generations.

Many of these remedies are now supported by modern scientific research, underscoring their efficacy.

**In Africa**, traditional healing often blends spirituality with herbal medicine, recognising the interplay of community, nature, and ancestors in personal well-being.

Plants such as rooibos (for antioxidants) and devil's claw (for inflammation) are widely used, reflecting a deep respect for the land's healing power.

**In the Americas,** indigenous healing traditions emphasise the sacredness of plants, rituals, and spiritual practices. The use of sage for smudging, cacao ceremonies, and sweat lodges are examples of how these cultures integrate physical and spiritual cleansing to promote health and balance.

When we integrate these global practices, we enrich our own journeys toward self-healing, strengthen our connection to the divine, and nurture inner harmony. Embracing a multicultural approach to wellness allows us to honour the wisdom of our ancestors while creating a more holistic and balanced future.

Naturopathy, as I have come to understand it, is more than just a health practice, it is a way of being. It is about treating the body as a sacred temple, respecting and honouring the food we eat, and valuing the earth we walk upon. While this way of life may not suit everyone, the principles at its core, gratitude, mindfulness, and respect for the interconnectedness of all living things, are universal truths that can guide anyone toward a more harmonious existence.

Through the wisdom of global traditions, I have discovered many paths that lead back to the same truth: No one is broken, we are already whole. The simplicity of Japanese living, the balance of Ayurvedic practices, the rich herbal knowledge from European traditions, and the holistic insights from Western naturopathy, all point to the same divine connection of loving-kindness

## *How Does Pendulum Dowsing Work?*

Everything in the universe is energy, and our bodies are no exception. Pendulum dowsing taps into this energy field, aligning it with your higher consciousness. By holding the pendulum and asking specific questions, you invite subtle vibrations to guide its movements.

The pendulum might swing clockwise, counterclockwise, or side-to-side, with each motion indicating a unique response.

To begin, practitioners calibrate their pendulum by establishing baseline movements for "yes," "no," and other answers.

This calibration is deeply personal, making the pendulum a unique tool for connecting with spiritual energies and your higher self.

## *Why Use a Pendulum for Self-Healing?*

Pendulum dowsing is a powerful tool for self-healing because it brings you closer to your inner wisdom and divine support. By asking questions about your health and well-being, such as "Is this remedy right for me?" or "Do I need more rest today?" you align your choices with your body's unique needs and your highest good.

## *Benefits of Pendulum Dowsing in Self-Healing*

Pendulum dowsing strengthens your intuition, helping you trust your inner voice and deepen your understanding of your body's subtle signals. It offers personalised guidance, tailoring its responses uniquely to your energy and circumstances. It opens a channel to your Guardian Angel and higher self, creating a sacred space where divine wisdom can flow freely.

Beyond physical healing, dowsing can uncover emotional blockages and areas needing forgiveness or release, fostering greater peace and harmony. It also supports informed choices, helping you align your actions whether in choosing the right foods, supplements, or even daily activities with your energetic and spiritual needs.

## *How to Use a Pendulum in Self-Healing*

Create a sacred space where you can focus without distraction. Light a candle, play soft music, or simply call upon your Guardian Angel to join you, deepening your spiritual connection.

Take a few deep breaths and ground yourself by visualising roots growing from the soles of your feet into the earth. Feel yourself anchored, steady, and centred.

Set a clear intention for your session, such as gaining insight into your health or restoring emotional balance. Holding a strong, clear purpose will ensure your dowsing is aligned with your highest good.

Start by asking simple, specific yes-or-no questions like, "Will this supplement support my healing?" or "Should I prioritise rest today?" Watch the pendulum's movements gently and patiently, trusting the subtle energy responses you receive. If the answers seem unclear, rephrase your question with kindness and clarity.

At the end of your session, always express gratitude to your Guardian Angel, your higher self, and the divine for their loving support and guidance.

## *Choosing Your Pendulum*

The pendulum you choose should feel aligned with your energy and intentions. Different crystals carry unique vibrations.

Amethyst enhances intuition and promotes peace.

Clear Quartz amplifies energy and magnifies intentions.

Rose Quartz encourages self-love and emotional healing.

Black Tourmaline grounds your energy and provides strong protection.

Allow yourself to be drawn intuitively to the pendulum that feels right for you. Your heart will know.

## *Deepening Your Connection with Guardian Angels*

Pendulum dowsing is a beautiful way to build a deeper relationship with your Guardian Angel.

As you hold the pendulum and pose your heartfelt questions, you are not only seeking answers, you are opening a dialogue with the divine. You are learning to trust the gentle nudges, the unseen loving presence that has always surrounded you.

When you invite their guidance during your practice, you open yourself to their wisdom, comfort, and unconditional love. Pendulum dowsing thus becomes far more than a tool; it becomes a sacred act of devotion, a soft remembering of the truth that you are never alone.

You are exactly where you are meant to be. You always have been. And now, it is time to remember.

The intuitive practice of crystal pendulum dowsing has shown me how energy flows within and around us, revealing the unseen forces that guide our lives.

These practices remind us that self-healing is not about fixing what is broken but accepting we are returning to the wholeness that already exists within us.

Living this way is a spiritual journey, a divine invitation to align with our highest purpose. It teaches us to find peace in the present moment and staying present, to trust the path ahead even when it is unclear, and to embrace every lesson as a step toward greater understanding.

Every small choice we make in support of our well-being, whether it is eating nourishing food, spending time in nature, or cultivating a positive mindset, is a step closer to the unconditional love and harmony that is our birthright.

I have always felt accepted the quiet guidance of my Guardian Angel in this journey. It is a soft, intuitive voice that nudges me toward choices that nourish my body, mind, and spirit. I find joy and balance in being outdoors, breathing in the fresh air, feeling the warmth of the sun on my skin, and observing the ever-changing beauty of the seasons.

These moments ground me in the present, reminding me of the divine force that flows through all of life.

Whether I am walking through a forest, sitting by the ocean, listening to my grandchildren's fantastic stories or simply tending to my garden, I feel deeply connected to something greater than myself. Nature speaks in a language beyond words, and when we take the time to listen, we find that the answers we seek are already within us.

Practicing mindfulness and staying present is a daily choice, not always easy but always rewarding. Life can be overwhelming at times, especially as a holistic practitioner supporting others on their healing journeys my energy sometimes feels drained as I'm giving from my heart with unconditional love.

It is vital to nurture myself in return, to replenish my energy and ensure that I am giving from a place of abundance rather than depletion.

I hold firmly to the principle of treating others as I wish to be treated, sowing seeds of kindness and compassion wherever I go. In doing so, I have cultivated a beautiful harvest of loving relationships and friendships with like-minded souls who share this path of healing and connection.

Naturopathy, to me, is more than a practice, it is a sacred way of honouring the unity of body, mind, and spirit. It calls us to care for ourselves holistically, to listen to our inner wisdom, and to approach the world with mindfulness and sustainability. It is about understanding that every choice we make ripples through the greater tapestry of life, affecting not just ourselves but the world around us. From the food we choose to eat to the thoughts we allow to shape our minds, each decision carries energy and intention.

This journey of self-healing is also about embodying love in all that we do, not just self-love, but love for the earth, for others, and for the divine spirit that flows through all things. For me, this love is rooted in the teachings of Christ, in the compassionate way he moved through the world, offering kindness and healing to all.

It is a reminder that we are all connected, and that our purpose is not just to exist but to live fully, to love deeply, and to contribute to the greater good.

Spending time in nature remains one of the greatest gifts I give myself. It is in these quiet moments that I feel most aligned with my purpose, most connected to the Divine. The earth Gaia has always been my greatest teacher, showing me that growth takes time, that healing is a process, and that even in the face of challenges, there is always an opportunity to bloom.

And so, as I continue this path, I do so with an open heart and a curious mind, knowing that the journey itself is the destination. Every lesson, every experience, every connection is a stepping stone on the path of ascension.

I invite you to embrace this journey too, to listen to the wisdom within you, and to trust that the answers you seek are already there, waiting to be revealed. In the end, it is not about reaching some final state of perfection but about living in harmony with yourself, with others and with the world around you. It is about finding joy in the simple things, peace in the present moment, and love in every breath you take. This is the sacred journey of natural living and self-healing, a path that leads not just to personal transformation but to a deeper connection with the divine force that unites us all.

## *A Journey into Aromatherapy: A Spiritual Connection to Nature*

From my earliest days, I have been enchanted by the power of plants and their profound connection to the natural world. One of my first encounters with this magic occurred during a sunlit afternoon in my family garden.

My small hands instinctively reached for rose petals and lavender flowers, drawn not only by their beauty but by an energy I could feel radiating from them, a life force that seemed to whisper to my soul.

I gently gathered the fallen rose petals, careful not to disturb the blooms still adorning the bush and placed them in a simple jar of water. By the next morning, the water had transformed, infused with a delicate, heavenly aroma as if the roses themselves had breathed their love into it overnight. Lavender held a different kind of magic for me. I would tie its flowers into neat bundles as they dried, their fragrance growing more concentrated and potent with time. The scent was soothing yet vibrant, like a gentle embrace from nature itself, reminding me of something ancient and sacred.

Even as a child, I understood that these plants held an energy far beyond what my eyes could see. Being clairvoyant, I often glimpsed shimmering colours darting between the leaves, the playful movements of elementals or fairy spirits, guardians of these living treasures.

I always asked permission before picking flowers, feeling a silent, unseen presence guiding me, urging me to wait until the petals were just past their peak, radiating their final burst of beauty before returning to the earth.

Through these experiences, I came to understand that all plants hold a profound desire to honour the divine source of creation. Their vibrant colours, intoxicating aromas, and intricate structures are not just for survival, they are offerings to the world, reminders of the divine spark in every living thing. This early connection shaped a deep reverence for nature and its gifts, a reverence I have passed down to my children and Grandchildren, watching them find their own magic in the beauty of the natural world.

Our relationship with the Earth, Gaia, is not just about receiving her gifts. Gaia gives freely and abundantly, offering us nourishment, beauty, and healing, yet how often do we pause, to give back? As we harvest her blessings, it is our responsibility to pour divine unconditional love, gratitude, and healing energy back into the earth. We are not just passive recipients; we are caretakers and co-creators. Gaia is not separate from us; she is the very ground we walk upon, the air we breathe, the life force that sustains us.

She too is on her own journey of Ascension, and as we heal ourselves, we assist in her healing as well.

Instead of filling the earth with our worries, fears, and burdens, let us fill her with our love, laughter, and light. Let us imagine Gaia healthy and well, her forests thriving, her oceans clear, and her skies bright.

Every time we plant a seed, inhale the fragrance of a flower, or walk barefoot on her soil, we can offer her our unconditional love in return. In this sacred exchange, we foster not only our own Ascension but also the flourishing of the planet that cradles us in her arms.

## *Mother Nature Whispers*

It was a beautiful summer's day, the kind where the sky stretches wide and blue, and the warmth of the sun feels like the Earth herself is smiling.

My young daughters, their bright eyes sparkling with curiosity and wonder, came running to me, their voices full of excitement. "Mummy, can we pick some flowers for the house?" they asked, their little baskets already in hand.

I smiled, feeling the familiar tug of joy in my heart, but gently reminded them of something sacred. "Of course," I said softly, "but we must ask the flower fairies first."

Hand in hand, we wandered into the garden, the air rich with the scent of roses, geraniums, and the myriad blossoms that filled our little patch of Earth. The sun danced on the petals, casting jewels of light across the leaves. At each magnificent rose bush, each vibrant geranium, and every delicate bloom in between, we paused. Closing our eyes, we whispered the same heartfelt question to the flower fairies: *"May we take some flowers for our home? Please, we ask you to release the life source from each stem we touch."*

It wasn't just a ritual, it was a sacred act of respect, a moment of deep connection with the unseen magic of nature. We weren't merely picking flowers; we were acknowledging the life force that thrived within each bloom, the elemental spirits that gave them their beauty and vitality.

With secateurs in hand, and my daughters clutching their little baskets, they carefully selected their favourite flowers. Each cut was made with reverence, every bloom handled as though it were a precious gift. When we were finished, we brought them inside, arranging them delicately in vases. The colours of nature, blush pinks, fiery reds, sunny yellows, now brightened our home, filling every corner with their beauty and the sweet, heady scent of summer.

Then, something extraordinary happened. A brilliant kaleidoscope of colour shot through the rooms of our home, swirling and dancing in the air like living light. It was as if a thousand tiny rainbows had burst into being, shimmering and spinning with a life of their own. We stood frozen, hearts pounding with a mixture of awe and disbelief, our eyes wide as the dazzling lights weaved through the rooms.

Then, in the stillness that followed, we *heard* them, the flower fairies. Their voices were ethereal, like the delicate tinkling of tiny silver bells caught in a gentle breeze, clear yet impossibly soft. Their words floated to us, not with sound alone but with a feeling that wrapped around our hearts.

They told us they had followed the flowers, curious to see inside our home, to share in the beauty we had created. Now, they whispered, it was time to return to their own world.

My daughters were beside themselves with excitement, their faces alight with the pure, unfiltered joy that only children possess. They had seen it, the magic of the flower fairies, real, undeniable, and breathtakingly beautiful. Their laughter rang out like music as we dashed around the house, flinging open every window and door, ensuring that every little fairy could find its way back outside.

It felt like we were part of something ancient and sacred, a timeless dance between the human world and the elemental spirits of Gaia.

Even now, when I think back to that day, my heart swells with gratitude and wonder. It was more than just a summer's afternoon in the garden, it was a glimpse into the hidden magic that surrounds us, a reminder that the Earth is alive with spirit and that, if we listen closely, we might just hear it whisper back.

## *Uplifting and Soothing Aromatherapy*

In the realm of holistic self-healing, essential oils are revered as gifts from the earth, connecting our physical lives to the nurturing embrace of the spiritual. For those walking a spiritual path, these potent natural remedies offer more than physical benefits. Each oil carries a unique vibration that harmonises the body, mind, and spirit, fostering a deeper sense of connection with our Guardian Angels and the divine realms.

When used with mindful intention, essential oils open a sacred space within us, allowing for communion with the guiding energies that watch over us.

The simple act of inhaling their fragrance becomes a prayer, a bridge between the physical and the ethereal. However, while these oils hold powerful healing properties, it's essential to approach them with respect and care.

Consulting a healthcare provider or certified aromatherapist is crucial, particularly in specific situations like pregnancy, epilepsy, or when using oils for children and the elderly.

Beloved oils such as frankincense lavender lemon, rosemary orange, tea- tree and myrrh have been cherished for centuries, their timeless wisdom passed down through generations.

Yet even these familiar friends must be used responsibly. For instance, rosemary oil, known for its circulatory benefits, and citrus oils, which can heighten skin sensitivity to sunlight, require thoughtful use and caution. Accurate dilution, mindful diffusion, and testing for skin sensitivity are essential steps in cultivating a balanced aromatherapy practice those honours both the body and the spirit.

## *Creating Spiritual Blends for Healing and Connection*

As you explore the world of essential oils, remember that each drop carries nature's love and intention to nurture, heal, and uplift. When you create a blend with clear purpose and divine blessings, you infuse it with positive energy, transforming aromatherapy into a sacred ritual. Each blend becomes a personal offering, a way to connect with the healing wisdom of the earth and the guidance of the divine.

Here are some of my favourite blends that I have used over the years, each one crafted with love and reverence for the natural world: 30ml of any vegetable oil my favourite is almond soya bean avocado rich in vitamins carrier oils are plant-based oils used to dilute essential oils before applying them to the skin.

Essential oils are highly concentrated and can cause irritation or adverse reactions if applied directly, so carrier oils help "carry" the essential oils safely onto the skin. Besides dilution, carrier oils are packed with nutrients like vitamins, fatty acids, and antioxidants that nourish and protect the skin.

When choosing a carrier oil, consider your skin type and specific needs. For example, avocado oil is fantastic for deep hydration, while almond or peach kernel oil is great for sensitive or delicate skin. You can even mix carrier oils to create customised blends that cater to your unique skin concerns.

1. **Avocado Oil Rich in:**

   **Vitamin E:** A powerful antioxidant that helps protect the skin from environmental damage and promotes healing.

   **Vitamin D:** Supports skin cell growth and repair.

   **Vitamin A:** Helps in skin cell regeneration and improves skin texture.

   **Oleic Acid (Omega-9):** Deeply moisturizing, making it great for dry or mature skin.

   **Potassium & Lecithin:** Help nourish and hydrate the skin.

- **Best for:** Dry, mature, or sun-damaged skin. It's thick and penetrates deeply, making it ideal for deep hydration and soothing irritated skin.

2. **Sweet Almond Oil Rich in:**

   **Vitamin E:** Protects the skin from oxidative stress and keeps it soft and smooth.

   **Vitamin A:** Supports skin cell turnover, helping reduce fine lines.

   **Omega-6 Fatty Acids (Linoleic Acid):** Helps soothe and moisturize the skin.

   **Zinc:** Beneficial for healing minor skin irritations and acne.

- **Best for:** All skin types, especially sensitive or irritated skin. It's lightweight and absorbs quickly, making it a popular choice for massage oils.

**3. Soybean Oil Rich in:**

**Vitamin E:** Acts as an antioxidant, protecting skin from free radical damage.

**Omega-3 Fatty Acids:** Help reduce inflammation and support skin barrier health.

**Lecithin:** A natural emollient that softens and smooths the skin.

**Phytosterols:** Help maintain the skin's barrier and moisture balance.

❖ **Best for:** Combination or aging skin. It has a light texture and helps improve skin elasticity and smoothness.

**4. Peach Kernel Oil Rich in:**

**Vitamin E:** Helps keep the skin hydrated and protected from environmental damage.

**Vitamin A:** Encourages skin renewal and improves elasticity.

**Oleic Acid (Omega-9) and Linoleic Acid (Omega-6):** Provide moisture and support skin barrier health.

**Antioxidants:** Help combat premature aging and promote a radiant complexion.

❖ **Best for:** Sensitive, dry, or mature skin. It's light, non-greasy, and easily absorbed, making it ideal for facial oils.

**Anti-Aging Facial Oil Blend (50ml)**

*Ingredients:*

**Avocado Oil** – 20ml (deeply moisturizing, rich in vitamins A, D, and E)

**Sweet Almond Oil** – 20ml (lightweight, softens skin, rich in vitamin E)

**Shea Butter** – 8g (about 1.5 teaspoons) (intensely hydrating, rich in vitamins A and E)

**Neroli Essential Oil** – 10 drops (promotes cell regeneration, improves skin elasticity, and has a calming floral scent)

*Instructions:*

**Melt the Shea Butter:**

Place the shea butter in a small heatproof bowl and gently melt it using a double boiler (or place the bowl over a pot of simmering water). Stir occasionally until fully melted. Remove from heat [or buy already blended]

**Add Carrier Oils:**

Once the shea butter cools slightly but is still liquid, add the avocado oil and sweet almond oil. Stir well to combine.

**Add Essential Oil:**

Add 10 drops of neroli essential oil to the mixture. Stir gently to ensure its evenly distributed.

**Bottle the Blend:**

Pour the mixture into a **50ml dark glass bottle** or jar to protect the oils from light, which can degrade their potency. Let it cool completely before sealing the container.

**Label and Store:**

Label your blend with the ingredients and date. Store in a cool, dark place. This blend should last up to **6 months** if kept properly.

*How to Use:*

**Apply:** After cleansing your face, apply 3-4 drops of the blend to your fingertips and gently massage it into your skin using upward, circular motions. Focus on areas prone to fine lines like around the eyes, mouth, and forehead.

**Frequency:** Use it **morning and night** as part of your skincare routine. You can also layer it over your moisturiser for extra hydration, especially at night.

***Why This Blend Works for Aging Skin:***

**Avocado Oil** deeply penetrates the skin, delivering essential nutrients and stimulating collagen production.

**Sweet Almond Oil** softens the skin and improves elasticity, helping to smooth fine lines.

**Shea Butter** locks in moisture and provides a protective barrier, helping to plump the skin.

**Neroli Essential Oil** is known for its rejuvenating properties, promoting cell regeneration and giving the skin a natural glow.

This blend is rich, yet absorbs well, leaving your skin feeling soft, nourished, and radiant. It's a beautiful, natural way to support aging skin with love and care!

## *General Benefits of Carrier Oils:*

- **Dilution of Essential Oils:** Make essential oils safe to apply to the skin.
- **Nourishment:** Provide vitamins and fatty acids that nourish and protect the skin.
- **Moisturisation:** Help lock in moisture, leaving the skin soft and smooth.
- **Skin Barrier Support:** Strengthen and protect the skin's natural barrier.

## *Some of my most favourite recipes*

**Sleep and Relaxation Blend**

- Valerian 6 drops calming promotes restful sleep
- Chamomile 4 drops soothing reduces anxiety
- Cedarwood 4 drops grounding induces relaxation.

**Anxiety Relief Blend**

- Neroli 5 drops uplifting reduces stress
- Ylang Ylang 5 drops calming lowers heart rate
- • Frankincense 4 drops grounding promotes inner peace.

**Revitalising Blend**

- Maychang 6 drops energising awakens the senses
- Rosemary 6 drops enhance focus and memory
- Lemon 4 drops refreshing uplifting.

**Concentration Blend**

- Black Pepper 6 drops stimulating sharpens mental clarity
- Lavender 6 drops balancing soothes the mind
- Sandalwood 4 drops grounding connects to the spiritual

## *A Spiritual Partnership with Nature*

As you embrace aromatherapy, let it be more than just a healing practice. Let it remind you of your sacred connection to Gaia and the divine creation all around you. Trust your intuition, listen to the whispers of your heart, and follow the gentle guidance of your Guardian Angel as you blend the ancient wisdom of essential oils with your personal intentions. Each mindful breath becomes an invitation to experience love, healing and sacred connection.

With every blend, every inhalation of a heavenly aroma, you honour the profound partnership between yourself and the divine. May this sacred practice guide you toward a life of balance, harmony, and joy, aligned with the rhythms of nature and the infinite grace of the universe.

Remember, you are never alone on this journey. Every plant, every drop of oil, and every spirit of nature is here to support and uplift you, reminding you of the abundant love that surrounds you always. As you care for yourself, you care for the Earth. As you heal, Gaia heals with you. Together, you rise in love and light, co-creating a world filled with beauty, compassion, and infinite joy.

In this sacred dance with nature, honour the preciousness of what you hold. Each drop of essential oil is a treasure a single drop of Rose Absolute requires the tender devotion of over 3,000 petals. Within every bottle lies the concentrated spirit of countless blooms, offered in pure love and service to your healing and growth.

May you use each drop with reverence, gratitude, and mindful intention, cherishing the deep spiritual partnership between yourself, the Earth and divine creation.

*Beautiful English Oak Tree*

CHAPTER 7

# Esoteric Cleansing – Revitalising Tools

## *Awakening to Your Divine Energy*

Esoteric cleansing is the sacred practice of purifying not just the physical body, but the unseen layers of our being our aura, our emotions, our spirit, and our connection to the Divine. It honours the understanding that we are more than flesh and bone; we are intricate beings of energy, sensitive to the unseen currents that flow around us and within us.

Throughout life, we naturally collect energies some uplifting, others heavy or discordant. Without regular cleansing, these unseen burdens can cloud our intuition, weigh down our spirit, and create a feeling of disconnection from our inner light.

Esoteric cleansing is the loving act of releasing these energies with sacred intention, restoring the purity of our energy field and realigning us with our true divine nature. It is a way of coming home to the soul remembering who we truly are beneath the layers of experience, expectation, and worldly noise.

In the quiet moments of your day, have you ever felt a soft longing, a gentle pull towards something greater? Perhaps it is a whisper in your heart, a knowing that there is more to life than what meets the eye a desire to understand yourself more deeply, to experience a peace that lingers, to align with something vast and beautiful.

This is the call of your soul, an invitation to awaken once more to your radiant, infinite self.

For me, the path of ascension has been slow, unfolding like the petals of a flower opening to the morning sun. Through years of guiding healing sessions, leading heartfelt workshops, and embracing holistic practices, I have given my energy away freely with unconditional love. However, there have been times when I have felt deeply drained.

This is the work of what I call energy parasites individuals or energies that, knowingly or *unknowingly, draw* vitality from others.

My Guardian Angel, Mena, would often offer symbols of protection and an inner knowing when something was not in alignment with my highest good.

Recognising energy parasites is not about judgement, but about self-preservation. Some people, environments, or even thought-forms can act as siphons, leaving us depleted. Protecting ourselves energetically is an act of sacred self-respect, a way to honour the divine within.

I have been blessed to witness countless souls begin this sacred journey. Some arrive with weary hearts, longing for renewal, while others come with quiet curiosity, drawn towards something they cannot yet name. No matter where their journey begins, they all share the same deep yearning to return home to themselves, to rediscover their authentic essence, and to find peace in the gentle embrace of the universe.

Each journey is unique, yet we are all connected by a common thread, the need to cleanse, refresh, and realign our energy fields. Just as we nurture our bodies with rest and nourishment, so too must we tend to our spirits with care and devotion. Without conscious energy cleansing, we may carry lingering emotions, energetic imprints, and unseen burdens that weigh us down, dimming the brilliance of our inner light.

Through spiritual cleansing, we create space for renewal, clarity, and divine connection. We open our hearts to deeper wisdom, we strengthen our intuition, and we welcome peace that soothes the soul. When our energy is clear and flowing freely, we hear the loving whispers of our Guardian Angels more easily, sense the divine walking with us, guiding us, holding us in every moment.

The practices within this chapter are offered with love. They are here to support you, to uplift you, and to remind you that you are never alone.

Esoteric cleansing is more than a ritual; it is a tender act of self-love, a way of honouring the sacred light within you. It is a way of coming home to yourself again and again.

Take a gentle breath. Place a hand over your heart and reflect:

What does it feel like to be in harmony with your authentic essence?

Can you remember a time when you felt truly aligned with your higher self?

## *Signs That Your Energy Needs Cleansing*

Just as the physical body gives us signals when it needs rest, nourishment, or healing, so too does our energetic body speak to us. If you have been feeling particularly drained, overwhelmed, or disconnected, these may be signs that your energy field is asking for cleansing.

**Some common indicators are:**

- A persistent feeling of heaviness or fatigue, even after rest
- Frequent mood swings, anxiety, or unexplained sadness
- Difficulty concentrating or feeling mentally foggy
- A sense of being emotionally or spiritually blocked
- Feeling drained after interactions with certain people or environments
- Frequent negative thoughts, self-doubt, or a sense of being weighed down

## *Understanding Energy Parasites*

In the unseen world of energy, not all interactions are nurturing. Some individuals, knowingly or unknowingly, act as energy parasites, feeding off the light and vitality of others. These draining connections may manifest through persistent negativity, emotional manipulation, or a constant need for attention.

As empaths and lightworkers, we are especially sensitive to these subtle energetic imbalances. Recognising them is not about blame, but about loving awareness. By becoming conscious of where our energy flows, we can protect our sacred light and strengthen our inner resilience.

Your energy is precious. Guard it with love and compassion.

## *Sacred Cleansing Techniques for the Human Aura and Spirit*

There are many gentle ways to cleanse and revitalise your energy field, drawing upon the blessings of nature, sacred tools and divine light Here is a small list of the most popular When guided by higher intelligence your Guardian Angel will is by your side. Make space to listen.

### Smudging with White Sage

White sage has long been honoured for its powerful cleansing properties. As the sacred smoke rises, it carries away stagnant energies, restoring clarity and peace.

To use: Light a bundle of white sage, allowing the flame to catch for a moment before blowing it out. Gently waft the smoke around your body, starting from your feet and moving upwards. Visualise any heaviness dissolving into the air.

Affirm softly as you smudge:

"I cleanse my body, mind, and spirit of all energies that no longer serve my highest good."

### The White Flame of a Candle

The flame of a candle is a symbol of the eternal divine light that lives within us all.

To use: Light a white candle with clear intention. Sit quietly, gazing into the flame. Visualise its pure white fire expanding, surrounding and filling you with luminous energy, burning away all that is heavy or unclear.

Affirm gently:

"I am illuminated by the pure flame of the Divine. All that is not of light is released and transformed."

### Salt: Earth's Ancient Purifier

Salt is a natural purifier, a gift from Gaia herself, grounding and protective.

To use: Place small bowls of pure sea salt in the corners of your home to absorb negativity. Alternatively, add salt to a warm bath to cleanse your aura deeply. You may also trace a small circle of salt around you when meditating for added protection.

Affirm as you work with salt:

"I am grounded, purified, and protected by the sacred gifts of the Earth."

### Invoking the Holy Trinity

Calling upon the Holy Trinity brings the highest vibration of divine love and protection into your space.

To use: Bring your hands together in prayer and with sincere heart, speak:

"In the name of the Father/Mother, the Son/Daughter, and the Holy Spirit, I call forth divine protection, healing, and purification. Fill me with Your sacred light."

Feel yourself surrounded by the luminous embrace of the Holy Trinity, deeply safe and blessed.

## *Symbols of Protection through the Ages*

Throughout time, sacred symbols have been called upon to protect, strengthen, and guide the soul. They serve as beacons of light, connecting us with the divine and reminding us that we are never truly alone.

**Some of the most powerful protective symbols include:**

- **The Cross** — a symbol of divine love and everlasting protection, aligning us with the Holy Trinity.
- **The Eye of Horus** — an ancient emblem of healing and safe-guarding, often used to protect against negativity.
- **The Pentacle** — representing balance and the unity of the elements, creating a circle of sacred space and spiritual strength.
- **The Hamsa Hand** — a universal sign of protection against harm, inviting blessings and divine favour.
- **The Ankh** — the Egyptian key of life, offering spiritual continuity and eternal safeguarding of the soul.
- **The Triple Spiral (Triskele)** — a Celtic symbol reflecting life's cycles and protecting the spirit through all transitions.

You may find yourself drawn to one or more of these symbols. Trust your intuition. Carry them as amulets, wear them as jewellery, place them on your altar, or simply visualise them when you seek added strength. When used with heartfelt intention, these sacred symbols can create a powerful shield of light around your being.

# *Deflecting Harmful Energy*

## The Importance of Protecting Against Electromagnetic Interference

When I first learned about the potential harmful effects of electromagnetic frequencies also known as EMFs, I felt a deep responsibility to protect myself and those I care about. I had been suffering from headaches dry eyes and unexplained fatigue for quite some time. I assumed it was simply the result of spending long hours in front of a computer screen. However, my Guardian Angel seemed to be at work showing me unexplained coincidences through newsfeeds on my online holistic health and well-being links.

These gentle nudges made me pause and wonder if there might be more to my symptoms than I realised. This inner prompting led me to explore the invisible energy that surrounds us every day and how it might be impacting our health.

As someone who has always valued natural remedies and the healing power of crystals, I turned to smoky quartz which is known for its grounding and protective properties. I placed it near my computer at work and my phone at home hoping to shield myself from the EMFs emitted by these devices. I also discovered energy dots small, yet powerful tools designed to harmonise the frequencies from electronic devices and reduce their impact on the body.

Encouraged by the results I began sharing these tools with others urging them to take small steps to protect themselves.

## A Gift from Gaia: Finding Black Obsidian

One cold, crisp winter's day, my husband and I embarked on a walk through the local woods, seeking solace in nature. We crossed a muddy field, the damp earth clinging to our boots as we pressed forward. The air was sharp and fresh, filling my lungs with a sense of renewal. The world around us felt hushed, as though nature herself was waiting for something sacred to unfold.

As we walked, something caught my husband's eye a glimmer in the soil, a faint shimmer that seemed to call to us. He bent down, brushed away the earth, and handed me a smooth, cool piece of black obsidian. It was a beautiful gift, placed before me as though Gaia herself had answered a silent prayer.

My Guardian Angel, Mena, had often told me that black obsidian would help balance my energy and dispel negativity. She had advised me to place one piece on my crown chakra, two on my root chakra, and one near my computer for protection. Until that moment, I had been searching for the missing pieces. Now, Gaia had lovingly provided.

I held the stone to my heart and whispered a quiet thank you to the universe. After cleansing the obsidian with pure water and clear intention, I placed it as Mena had instructed. Almost immediately, I felt a profound shift. The sluggishness I had been carrying lifted, a renewed vitality coursed through me, and my thoughts became clear once more.

The black obsidian had arrived exactly when I needed it most, a sacred reminder that we are always supported when we trust and remain open to receive.

### The Power of Nature's Energy Cleansing

Nature itself is one of our greatest healers. Walking barefoot upon the earth, known as earthing, allows us to reconnect with Gaia's stabilising energy.

Trees offer steadfast support, dissolving emotional heaviness when we stand close, place our hands on their bark, or simply sit beneath their branches. Place hands palms down on the earth sending excess energy into her with love.

Water is a powerful cleanser the sound of a river, the touch of ocean waves, or the flow of warm water over your skin in the shower can wash away energetic debris. Even the wind plays its part, carrying away stagnant energies and uplifting the spirit with its lively touch.

Simply being present with nature's elements can transform your energy field, restoring balance and bringing you home to yourself.

## *A Closing Ritual: Sealing Your Sacred Energy*

After cleansing, it is important to seal your aura with love and divine protection, ensuring that the light you have nurtured remains strong and radiant.

Find a quiet space. Close your eyes and place your hands over your heart. Breathe deeply, and visualise a soft golden light forming a bubble of protection all around you radiant, strong, and loving.

Call upon Archangel Michael. Imagine his electric blue light descending from above, fortifying your golden bubble with powerful, unwavering strength.

Invoke the violet flame of Saint Germain. See a swirling violet fire within your golden bubble, transmuting any lingering negativity into pure light and love.

Softly affirm:

"I am a being of golden light, protected and whole.

Archangel Michael shields me with electric blue strength.

The violet flame of Saint Germain purifies and uplifts my soul.

I release all energies that are not mine with love and grace.

I stand rooted in my divine power, radiant, sovereign and free."

Feel your energy field sealing with love, light, and divine grace, shimmering around you like a shield of purest energy.

CHAPTER 8

# The Connection Between Animals and the Divine

I have always believed that animals hold a special place in the divine order. I've seen their light, diming literally as they pass from this world. In those tender moments, I've felt the presence of their Guardian Angel, a comforting over-lighting presence guiding their soul with love. This experience has deepened my understanding of the sacred bond we share with animals and reminded me that they are as much a part of the divine creation as we are.

The idea that animals have angels watching over them feels so natural to me. Angels as protectors and messengers extends their love and care to all living beings. I believe animals are wrapped in the same divine love that holds the entire universe together.

When it comes to whether animals have souls, I think they absolutely do. Different traditions explore this idea in their own ways. Christianity speaks of a "nephesh," a life force that animals possess, while Hinduism and Buddhism see animals as part of the reincarnation cycle, their souls evolving through lifetimes. Indigenous teachings resonate deeply with me too, the belief that every animal has its own spirit or essence, a sacred part of the web of life. And of course, the way animals show emotion, loyalty and intelligence makes it impossible for me to think of them as anything less than soulful beings.

The idea of an animal heaven is such a comforting thought, isn't it? I love the vision of the Rainbow Bridge, where our beloved pets wait for us, tails wagging and hearts full of love. It's a beautiful way to imagine the continuation of the bond we share with them, a connection that transcends this physical life.

I often think about how animals fit into the spiritual world. Some traditions see them as part of symbolic kingdoms tied to the elements. For example, deer and elephants are said to embody the grounding energy of the earth, while birds and butterflies represent freedom and higher perspectives.

Then there are the wolves and eagles, whose powerful presence symbolises leadership, or mythical creatures like dragons, which inspire imagination and wisdom. To me, these ideas feel like ways to celebrate the unique energy and beauty that each animal brings into our lives.

Throughout history, animals have been revered in so many cultures. Cats were worshipped in Ancient Egypt, not only for their grace but for their role as protectors. Cows in Asia are honoured for their nurturing qualities, seen as symbols of abundance and peace. And closer to home, I've always loved the stories of lions representing strength and robins bringing messages of hope.

In Pagan traditions, animals are seen as equal partners in the sacred balance of life. They teach us lessons, guide us through challenges and connect us to the rhythms of the natural world. If it's the stag symbolising grace, the raven offering insight, or the hare reminding us of renewal, there's so much we can learn from them if we take the time to watch and listen.

I believe animals are here to teach us about love, compassion and the interconnectedness of life. They inspire us to live with kindness, humility and gratitude. They remind us that every moment is precious and that life, in all its forms, is a sacred gift.

When I look into the eyes of an animal, I feel the wonder of creation staring back at me. Their presence is a gentle reminder that we are all connected, all part of something greater. To respect animals is to honour life itself and that, to me, is one of the most beautiful ways we can express love and reverence for the divine.

## *Your Ability to Heal*

The ability to heal is a spiritual gift within each of us, waiting to be awakened through love and divine guidance. Healing does not require special skills, only a pure authentic heart, genuine intention and a willingness to allow your Guardian Angel to guide you with divine love and light.

Animals, with their sensitivity and unconditional love, respond readily to this energy. Every encounter, whether with a cherished pet or a wild animal, is a divine opportunity for connection and transformation.

## *Animal Healing with My Guardian Angel*

One of my most moving experiences involved my koi carp. The largest fish in my pond often leapt out, as if unhappy with its environment. One day, it lay lifeless on the grass. Guided by my Guardian Angel, I instinctively placed it in a bucket of ice-cold water. Miraculously, it survived. My Guardian Angel then instructed me to move it to a larger pond, where it could thrive. By listening to divine guidance, gave the koi a new chance at life.

Another touching, yet deeply heartbreaking, true story involved one of my farm kittens who was too young to care for her litter. Helpless and overwhelmed, she lost two of her babies. I remember the sorrow in her eyes as she gently carried the lone survivor to me, placing it at my feet as if pleading for help. My heart ached for her. In that moment, I felt guided by my Guardian Angel. I knelt beside them, placed my hands over their fragile bodies and allowed divine love to flow.

Something shifted. The mother kitten, who had been lost in grief and uncertainty, seemed to soften. Slowly, she accepted the healing presence around her and, as if awakened to her strength, embraced her baby once more. From that moment on, she nurtured her little one with unwavering love. They both went on to live a long and happy life with our family.

That experience taught me the profound power of listening to divine guidance, staying present in the moment and trusting the wisdom of my Guardian Angel. Even in the depths of loss, love has the power to heal, restore and bring light where there was once sorrow.

## *Animal Healing and Karma*

Karma, the spiritual principle of cause and effect, is deeply intertwined with our relationships with animals. These sacred beings often enter our lives to guide, teach, or heal us, serving as reflections of our own journey. A loyal dog may remind us of trust and faithfulness, while a persistent cat may teach us patience or resilience.

Even fleeting encounters with wild animals can carry symbolic messages, encouraging growth and renewal.

## *An unwanted lesson*

Cats have a way of teaching us lessons, even when we're not ready to see or learn them. I believe they tune into our souls, offering unconditional love in ways we may not immediately recognise.

A friend once told me she was annoyed by a cat that kept visiting her, refusing to leave despite her lack of attention. She was going through a difficult time and pushed the cat away, unwilling to accept its presence. I often wonder if she had opened her heart to the healing the cat offered, would her life have taken a different path? For she is an angry unhappy woman who blames everyone for the many tragedies in her life.

Another friend once shared a poignant story about a neighbourhood cat that persisted in visiting her, despite her reluctance to accept its affection. Over time, she realised the cat was teaching her about companionship, trust and the simple yet profound act of receiving love.

Another tale involved a friend grieving the sudden loss of her husband. Soon after, a tiny kitten appeared on her doorstep, a gift of comfort in her darkest moments. Though she initially resisted adopting the kitten, the little one stayed, becoming a cherished companion. I believe the kitten carried a lesson in resilience and the power of love to heal even the deepest sorrow.

Animals intuitive nature and boundless love create opportunities for healing and balance, reminding us of the deep interconnectedness of all life. By inviting your Guardian Angel into these relationships, you can deepen your awareness of the spiritual lesson's animals bring.

Your Guardian Angel plays a vital role in these karmic encounters, gently guiding you to recognise the lessons animals bring into your life. Whether through companionship, persistence, or unconditional love, they help us grow, heal, align with our higher selves. Pets help us process and release karmic energy.

Healing animals feels no different from healing myself. It is a deeply personal and profound act of love and every time I do it, I feel as though I am stepping into something truly sacred.

When I focus on the gentle, divine energy that flows through all living beings, I am reminded of the beauty and connection that surround us all.

When I sit with an animal to offer healing, it is not just about helping them feel better physically or emotionally. It is about honouring their spirit and the unique light they bring into my life and the world.

Every healing moment becomes an exchange of trust and love, a bond that flows straight from the heart.

I have found that the most important things are love, pure intention and asking for guidance from my Guardian Angel. I always begin by quieting my mind and focusing on the present moment, allowing compassion to fill my heart. When I call on my Guardian Angel for help, I feel their presence as a soft, loving light guiding me. It is comforting to know they are with me, amplifying the healing energy and ensuring it flows exactly where it is needed.

I do not believe animal healing requires any special skill; rather, it is about the intention to love with all your heart. Ask your Guardian Angel to open the sacred chamber of your heart. Simply holding space for the animal, offering them love and kindness, makes all the difference. Whether I place my hands near them, share a quiet moment together, or simply focus on sending them love, I trust that the energy flows naturally and perfectly.

Every time I connect with an animal this way, I feel as though I am being healed, too. It is as if we are sharing something far beyond words, a deep, divine connection that reminds me of the sacredness of all life. I know this is a gift, not just for the animal but for my own spirit and I am so grateful to experience it.

## *Create a Quiet Space for Channelling Divine Light*

Start by finding a calm and peaceful place where both you and the animal feel safe and comfortable. This space should be free from distractions, allowing the animal to relax and trust in your presence. Take a moment to observe the animal's energy, ensuring they feel at ease and that you are approaching them with care and gentleness.

Settle into this space and bring your attention inward. Close your eyes and take a few deep breaths, feeling the air as it flows gently in and out of your body. As you exhale, imagine releasing any tension or stress, allowing your mind and body to soften. Focus on the rhythm of your breath, letting it guide you into a calm and grounded state.

Picture the energy of love and peace filling you with every breath. Let go of any worries or distractions, trusting that this moment is a sacred opportunity for connection and healing. Feel yourself becoming fully present, your heart open and ready to receive divine guidance.

As you become grounded, allow the animal to approach or settle near you naturally, respecting their need for space and trust. Simply being in this shared, quiet moment can create a powerful bond, setting the stage for the healing energy to flow. This act of creating a safe and calm environment is the first step in offering healing to an animal, a gesture of love and respect that honours their unique spirit and the divine connection between you.

## *Invoke Your Guardian Angel*

Close your eyes and take a focused breath, letting yourself become calm and grounded. Call upon your Guardian Angel with an open and sincere heart. Say, *"Dear beautiful Guardian, please come to my aid in healing this animal. Guide me with your divine wisdom and love as I become a channel of healing energy."* Trust completely in their loving presence as you invite them to join you in this sacred moment.

As you call on your Guardian Angel, imagine a golden light beginning to flow from the divine source of love.

Picture this light gently entering through the crown of your head, filling your entire being with warmth, peace and deep compassion. Feel it moving softly down through your throat and into your heart, expanding with every breath. This golden light carries the essence of unconditional love, divine healing and boundless kindness. Allow it to flow through your arms and gather in your hands, where it becomes a soothing, radiant energy, ready to bring comfort and healing.

Now, as you focus on the animal, visualise this golden light flowing gently from your hands, wrapping around them like a warm embrace.

See it softly illuminating their body, dissolving any discomfort and restoring balance and harmony to their energy. Trust that this divine connection, infused with love and guided by your Guardian Angel, is creating the perfect space for healing to unfold.

Hold onto this beautiful moment, knowing that the love and light you are sharing is not only bringing comfort to the animal but also strengthening the sacred bond between you. Recognise that this exchange of energy is a gift, one that nurtures both the animal and your own spirit. Let gratitude fill your heart as you trust in the divine guidance that flows through you.

## *Focus on Specific Areas*

If you sense or are aware of a specific area of discomfort in the animal, bring your full attention to that spot with a heart full of love and a deep intention to bring comfort. Approach the moment with tenderness and kindness, allowing your hands to hover near or rest lightly over the area, always respecting the animal's boundaries and their need to feel safe.

Let your touch, or the space between your hands and their body, be infused with care and respect, creating an atmosphere of trust.

Close your eyes for a moment and take a steady, focused breath grounding and balancing yourself in the energy of compassion and divine love. Allow your mind to quiet and your heart to open fully to the sacred connection between you and the animal.

Imagine a warm, golden light flowing gently from the divine source of love through your body and into your hands. Picture this light as soft, nurturing and full of healing energy, wrapping the area of discomfort like a gentle embrace.

As you focus on this light, see it easing tension and soothing any pain. Imagine the divine golden light restoring balance and harmony to the area, gently dissolving any discomfort or stress. With every breath, visualise the healing energy becoming stronger, yet always gentle and comforting, flowing in perfect alignment with the animal's needs.

In your mind, silently offer words of kindness and reassurance, or softly speak to them aloud if it feels right. You might say, *"You are safe. You are loved. I am here with you. All is well."* Let these words flow naturally, allowing your love and care to create a space where the animal feels secure and supported.

Trust that the animal can feel your intentions and that your Guardian Angel is guiding the process. Let the energy flow without force, simply allowing the divine light to do its work in harmony with the animal's spirit. Whether you sense visible changes or subtle shifts, know that your loving presence is enough and that the connection you are offering is deeply meaningful.

When you feel the energy begin to settle, take a moment to thank the animal for their trust and the divine for the healing light that flows through you. Rest in the warmth of this shared moment, knowing that you have acted from a place of pure love and compassion.

## *Mutual love and respect*

When the healing session feels complete, take a moment to express heartfelt gratitude. Gently acknowledge the animal for their trust and openness in receiving your love and care.

If the animal is still near, you might softly say, "Thank you for allowing me to share this moment with you. Your presence is a blessing and I honour the light and beauty you bring to this world."

Then, turn your attention inward and thank your Guardian Angel for their loving guidance and support. In your heart, express appreciation for their presence and for helping you channel divine healing energy. You might say, "Thank you, my Guardian Angel, for your unwavering love and guidance. Thank you for helping me connect with this beautiful soul and for allowing me to be a vessel of healing and compassion."

Feel the warmth of love and gratitude expanding within you, like a gentle glow that fills your entire being. Let this gratitude flow outward, embracing the animal, your Guardian Angel and the divine source of all love. This closing gesture honours the sacredness of the experience, deepening the bond between you, the animal and the divine energy that connects all life.

## *Ground Yourself*

After completing the healing session, take a moment to reconnect with the earth and ground your energy. Close your eyes and imagine strong, sturdy roots growing from the soles of your feet, reaching deep into the soil. Visualise these roots anchoring you to the earth, providing stability and balance. Feel the earth's steady, nurturing energy flowing upward through the roots into your body, calming your mind and restoring your strength.

Once you feel fully grounded, take a few deep breaths, allowing yourself to return to the present moment. Have a glass of water to further anchor your energy and replenish your body.

## *Sit quietly for a few minutes and reflect on the experience.*

Consider the connection you shared with the animal, the guidance of your Guardian Angel and the love and healing energy that flowed through you. Express gratitude for the divine assistance and for the trust of the animal, honouring this sacred exchange.

## *Heart-warming Encounter of Healing*

A client who owned an animal rescue sanctuary asked me to help a horse named Amba. Abandoned after her owner's passing, Amba struggled with trust issues. With guidance from my Guardian Angel, I worked with the sanctuary team to reassure Amba of her worth and love. I noticed the beautiful guardian Angels standing beside one of the stable girls. Intuitively I asked the girl if she wanted to hold her hands over the horse. Instructing her to call to her Guardian Angel. The girl was of course a natural healer and Amba responded Over time the horse regained confidence and became a gentle companion for sensory-impaired children and the stable girl trained in equine chiropractic.

Another experience involved Dobbie, a rescue pit bull who had been abused and avoided all human contact. Through patience and divine guidance, I connected with Dobbie's energy, offering calm and unconditional love. Over weeks, he began to trust and eventually became a loyal and affectionate companion.

## *The Sacred Bond*

Animals are divine gifts, sent to bring healing, joy and spiritual lessons. They remind us of the love, connection and light that permeates all of creation. When you invite your Guardian Angel into these interactions, you deepen this sacred bond, fostering healing and growth for both you and the animals in your life.

May you always trust in the gentle power of love and the divine presence that flows through you.

As you open your heart to the animals you encounter, know that every act of kindness, every moment of connection and every offering of healing creates waves of light that extend far beyond what the eye can see. Healing is not only a gift you give it is a sacred exchange, one that nurtures both the giver and the receiver.

May you walk this path with compassion, knowing that you are never alone staying true to your authentic self.

Your Guardian Angel is always by your side, guiding your hands, your heart and your spirit as you share this divine energy. Every time you offer healing; you are not only bringing comfort to an animal but also deepening your own connection to the sacredness of life itself.

It is my heartfelt hope you feel inspired to embrace your role as an animal and self - healing, guided by love and divine light. Together, you and the animals you encounter can create ripples of healing and connection that enrich your lives and the world.

*My beautiful cat*

CHAPTER 9

# Living Spiritually in the 21$^{st}$ Century

Lately, I have been thinking a lot about how artificial intelligence is changing the world and more importantly, how it is changing us. Everywhere I turn, I see AI making life easier, faster and more efficient. It can write, create and even "think" in ways we once believed were uniquely human. That leaves me wondering: what happens to our own creativity, intuition and inner wisdom when we lean too heavily on machines?

I have felt it myself the temptation to let technology do the work, the creeping sense that if I do not pause and engage with my own thoughts, something essential might slip away. AI is powerful, but if we are not mindful, we risk letting it dull our imagination and weaken our creative connection to something deeper. The divine spark that makes us conscious evolving beings.

However, I do not believe AI has to be the enemy of creativity or spirituality. If we use it with intention, as a tool rather than a master we can harness its power to expand our minds rather than replace them. AI can help us explore innovative ideas, spark inspiration and even deepen our understanding of ourselves and the world around us.

Living with spirit in the 21st century is about balance walking the delicate line between progress and ancient wisdom, between the tangible and the unseen. When we align body, mind and soul, we create a life of harmony, purpose and joy. The question is not whether AI will shape the future. The real question is: how will we choose to shape ourselves in this new world?

## *The Enduring Wisdom of Madame Blavatsky*

I first discovered Madame Helena Petrovna Blavatsky's teachings many years ago through spiritual development workshops. It was the 1970s, a time of great awakening and yet her name stood out to me as something far beyond the teachings of that era. Even then, I sensed she carried something ancient, profound and timeless.

Now, as humanity steps into a new age of frequency healing, vibrational medicine and self-mastery, her wisdom is more important than ever. I see her standing beside the great spiritual visionaries of all time her name as significant as Alice Bailey's, both women pioneers carrying keys to humanity's evolution.

For me, as a clairvoyant empath and energy healer, her work became a bridge between the unseen and the tangible, between spirit and matter, mysticism and science. What I had always felt intuitively suddenly became grounded real, undeniable.

Blavatsky was a woman far beyond her time. Born on August 12, 1831, in Yekaterinoslav, Russia (now Dnipro, Ukraine), she lived an extraordinary life, devoted to unveiling the hidden spiritual laws that govern existence. She passed away on May 8, 1891, in London, England leaving behind a legacy that the world is only now ready to embrace.

She foresaw a time when humanity would reclaim its divine power a time when we would awaken to the truth that self-healing, frequency alignment and energetic mastery are not just mystical ideas but our birthright.

That time is now.

## *Blavatsky's Teachings: No Boundaries to Healing*

Blavatsky did not belong to one tradition, one religion, or one philosophy. She travelled the world, studying with Tibetan monks,

Hindu sages, Kabbalists and Egyptian mystics. She was a seeker of the ancient truths long hidden from the Western world.

In 1875, she co-founded the Theosophical Society in New York, a movement dedicated to revealing the universal spiritual wisdom that underlies all teachings. Through her seminal works, The Secret Doctrine and Isis Unveiled, she revealed knowledge that defied the limitations of religion, science and materialism.

She taught that there are no boundaries to self-healing no limits to human expansion no restrictions on consciousness itself.

Blavatsky foresaw a world where humanity would rise above fear reclaim their spiritual sovereignty and embrace vibrational medicine as the key to self-healing. We are living in that world now.

As custodians of Gaia, our sacred planet, we are called to restore balance within ourselves, within the Earth and within the energetic fabric of existence. Self-healing and planetary healing are the same. As we raise our vibration, we elevate the consciousness of the entire planet.

## *Blavatsky's Vision of Frequency and Multidimensional Reality*

Blavatsky described reality as a vast spectrum of vibratory energy, where everything matters, thought and consciousness exists as frequency.

She revealed seven cosmic planes of existence each offering pathways for transformation, healing and awakening:

1. The Physical Plane-The material world of form, action and sensory experience.
2. The Astral Plane-The realm of emotions, desires and the energetic body.
3. The Mental Plane-The world of thought, imagination and manifestation.

4. The Buddhic Plane-The dimension of divine love, intuition and spiritual wisdom.
5. The Atmic Plane-The higher will, soul's purpose and spiritual leadership.
6. The Monadic Plane-The realisation of unity between individual and universal consciousness.
7. The Divine Plane -The highest realm of pure light, infinite awareness and divine connection.

She taught that spiritual evolution is a process of raising one's vibrational frequency, moving from the denser material world toward higher states of awareness and enlightenment.

Unlike traditional religious teachings that emphasised separation from the divine, Blavatsky insisted that we are divine beings capable of awakening our latent spiritual abilities, accessing higher wisdom and healing ourselves through vibrational alignment.

We do not need to seek healing outside of ourselves the power is already within us.

## *Blavatsky and the Power of Healing Frequencies*

Blavatsky knew what modern science is only now beginning to prove, that sound, thought and frequency directly influence our health, emotions and consciousness.

She anticipated that the key to health, vitality and enlightenment lay in the vibrational fields of energy that surround and sustain us.

## *The Power of Healing Frequencies*

Everything in the universe is energy, vibrating at different frequencies. Ancient wisdom and modern science both confirm that healing frequencies can restore balance, raise consciousness and facilitate deep spiritual awakening.

Blavatsky's teachings align with the Solfeggio frequencies, powerful sound waves known to promote healing: rediscovered as powerful healing tools:

- 396 Hz - Releases fear and subconscious guilt.
- 417 Hz - Removes negative energy and facilitates transformation.
- 528 Hz - Repairs DNA and activates cellular healing.
- 639 Hz - Balances relationships and harmonises the heart centre.
- 741 Hz - Detoxifies the body and mind.
- 852 Hz - Awakens intuition and spiritual perception.
- 936 Hz - The miracle tone, which activates divine consciousness. Blavatsky spoke of the illusion of separation the great forgetting of humanity's connection to Source.
- 936 Hz - The Frequency of Divine Awakening

936 Hz - is the frequency that dissolves this illusion.

- It activates the crown chakra, awakening our direct link to divine consciousness.
- It restores memory of our true self as infinite, limitless and part of the whole.

It bridges the gap between physical reality and spiritual truth. 936 Hz is often called the *miracle tone* because it is believed to reconnect us with our higher self, universal wisdom and pure divine love. This sacred frequency is deeply linked to the crown chakra, which governs spiritual awareness and our ability to experience oneness with all that is. It is a frequency of wholeness, peace and enlightenment, allowing us to rise above fear and reconnect with the eternal light within.

Many who meditate with 936 Hz experience profound inner peace, heightened intuition and spontaneous healing.

Blavatsky's work foretold this very phenomenon, that humanity would rediscover vibrational medicine, self-healing and energetic mastery. Today we see this truth unfolding in holistic healing, sound therapy and energy medicine. Her wisdom was a prophecy. We are now the generation that fulfils it.

## *Embracing Blavatsky's Teachings in the 21st Century*

Her legacy is more than just philosophy it is a call to action.

Blavatsky's teachings remind us that:

- Healing begins within.
- We are responsible for our own energy and well-being.
- Raising our personal vibration uplifts the entire planet.
- Science and spirituality are not separate together, they reveal the truth of energy and creation.

She knew that one day, spirituality and science would merge and today, quantum physics confirms her insights, which thought creates reality, energy shapes matter and frequency governs all life.

She was a visionary ahead of her time and now, at last, humanity is ready.

Blavatsky's message to us is clear:

Take responsibility for your own healing.

Align your vibration with truth and love.

Remember you are far greater than what the physical world alone reveals.

As we reconnect with her wisdom, let us honour Gaia, our sacred planet.

As we raise our own frequency, we uplift the entire collective fulfilling the prophecy of a higher vibrational humanity.

## *AO Scan™ – Advanced Technology*

Loran Swensen is the founder of Solex, established in 2021. Driven by a personal quest to support his son's health, he developed the AO Scan Mobile non-invasive device that utilizes bio resonance technology to monitor and balance the body's frequencies.

Swensen's work reflects a commitment to integrating advanced technology with holistic wellness practices, empowering individuals to take charge of their health through energy-based assessments. Solex

For more information, visit the Solex official website.

Throughout my years as a holistic healer, I have witnessed the quiet yet profound transformation that sound frequency as a healing aid can bring. I use AO Scan™ technology not just as a tool but as a bridge. A bridge that reconnects people to their own bodies, to their subtle energies and to the divine intelligence within.

This is not theory to me. My belief in energy, vibration, and frequency healing wasn't born from books or science journals. It came from an authentic, soul-deep knowing shaped by my own journey through illness, intuition, and spiritual awakening. As a clairvoyant, I see the subtle energies that move through people their auras, their light, the colours of their thoughts and how certain frequencies ripple through them. Some frequencies bring harmony, others, disruption and some miracles.

### Testament to bio frequencies as a aid for healing

In 2023, following the compulsory coronavirus vaccine, I began to experience a strange and relentless fatigue that came in heavy, crashing waves, particularly in the colder months. There were mornings I would wake with a weight so dense in my body that even brushing my hair felt like a monumental task. It was as though my energy had vanished into mist. I remember lying in bed, wondering how I would make it through the day. In that stillness somewhere between despair and surrender I turned inward and upward.

It was during one of my acupuncture sessions with the incredible Julia Hart that my life changed. She introduced me to bio- resonance and I can only describe the experience as mind-blowing. I was in awe barely believing that there was technology, an app, composed of algorithms that could attune to my body through sound and vibration.

I was hooked. My bio resonance journey with AO Scan™ began.

For me this was no ordinary healing method. This was medicine from the future guided by ancient wisdom and tuned to the unique frequency of my soul. Here's what became part of my daily healing ritual:

- AO Scan™ frequencies, precisely tuned to my body's needs
- Affirmations and divine messages from my Guardian Angels
- Daily meditation and conscious intention-setting, wrapped in love and surrender

**The Language of Healing Through Sound**

Using AO Scan™, I could analyse the frequencies in my voice and receive personalised tones crafted to restore balance, clarity, and vitality at the cellular level. These weren't generic soundscapes.

These were deeply intelligent vibrations, speaking the language of *me,* of my cells, my heart, my spirit.

There were days when I felt too depleted to move, too foggy to think. Yet after listening to my frequencies just a few minutes of sound tailored specifically for me something would shift.

My breath deepened.

My nervous system softened.

My thoughts cleared.

A quiet strength returned.

Even Julia, my acupuncturist, has been amazed. There is a renewed light in my eyes, a vitality that flows despite what my body has endured. I know with all my heart it is the power of frequency of sound, of aligning ourselves with healing frequencies, and keeping our hearts and minds open. There have been moments that felt nothing short of miraculous sound Is not only medicine It Is the future of medicine

I believe this with every fibre of my being: sound frequencies is not just an alternative therapy it is the future of healing.

We are vibrational beings. Every cell, every emotion, every thought has a frequency. When those frequencies fall out of tune through stress, trauma, toxins, or spiritual disconnection illness can arise. But when we realign with harmony, healing flows.

AO Scan™ has become a beloved part of my own healing and the support I offer to others. It is a reminder that we are not separate from our healing journey we are participants in it. We are creators of it.

**A Vision Held in My Heart**

I was given the vision of a sanctuary where modern and traditional medicine meld together giving humanity a beautiful place for recovery from dis-ease. A sacred healing space where frequency sound, acupuncture, energy work, and spiritual guidance come together perfectly.

A place to be healed and reassured no one is broken. This vision is not just for me.

It is my prayer my dream that these healing modalities become available to everyone.

Not just to the few, but to the many. It is my deepest hope to see a sanctuary on every corner, in every town.

Places of light, where frequency healing, compassion, and natural therapies are as common as pharmacies or coffee shops.

Places where people walk in burdened, and walk out lighter and free as they have remembered reconnected to their soul, their body, and the love that has never left them. These are the spaces our world is longing for, Healing Sanctuaries of wholeness, not just wellness.

It is probably already established in other Countries but not here in the UK as yet. I will hold this vision clearly in my heart nurturing it with intention, walking it gently into being, step by sacred step, nurturing with love and clarity until it finds its way into form.

## *The Spiritual Power of Fasting*

### Cleansing the Body, Awakening the Soul

Fasting, when practiced with intention and reverence, becomes far more than a physical detox. It is a sacred pause a clearing of inner space that invites deeper connection to the divine. Across cultures and spiritual traditions, fasting has long been honoured as a practice of purification, clarity, and communion with something greater than the self.

When the body is given rest from constant digestion, something miraculous begins to happen. Energy that was once used for breaking down food is redirected to healing, restoring, and renewing. The senses become sharper. The mind slows and expands. The soul begins to speak.

Fasting peels away distractions physical, mental, emotional and reveals what lies beneath. In that quiet, something sacred is remembered: we are more than our bodies, more than our cravings, more than our routines. We are spiritual beings, and fasting is one way to return to that truth.

Throughout time, those called to sacred service high priestesses, priests, oracles, shamans, and healers honoured fasting and purification as essential spiritual disciplines.

They understood that to perform divine works, the mind and body must be kept clear, grounded, and free of toxins. A pure vessel was required to receive divine insight, channel energy, and commune with Spirit.

`Their practices remind us that spiritual clarity begins with physical and energetic cleanliness. By releasing what weighs us down, we make space for what uplifts us. When we empty, we become open, receptive. radiant.

Fasting need not be extreme or overwhelming to be powerful. A simple one day fast, practiced with mindfulness and loving-compassion, can bring a sense of inner lightness, heightened intuition, and renewed energy.

When approached with love, fasting becomes an offering to your higher self, to your body temple, and to the divine intelligence that breathes through all of life.

### A Gentle Word of Caution

Fasting is a personal journey and like any sacred practice, it requires deep listening. If you are pregnant, nursing, managing chronic illness, recovering from disordered eating, or under medical care, it's important to speak with a qualified health practitioner before beginning a fast.

Fasting is not about punishment or restriction it is about clarity, devotion, and healing. Always honour your body's signals. There is no shame in modifying or postponing your fast. The path of healing is not linear, and kindness must walk alongside every step.

## *A Beginner's Simple Fast*

### One Day of Gentle Reset

This one-day fast is designed to be gentle, nourishing, and spiritually supportive. It allows your body to rest, your mind to quiet, and your intuition to sharpen all while offering you a deeper sense of connection to your higher self.

### The Day Before – Preparation

Begin to slow down. Choose plant-based, light foods that support digestion and energy.

Eat:

- Fresh fruits and vegetables
- Herbal teas
- Whole grains like quinoa, millet, or brown rice

Avoid:

- Heavy, processed foods
- Refined sugars
- Dairy and animal products
- Caffeine and alcohol

**Spiritual Prep:**

- Set a sacred intention.

  Ask yourself:

  *"What do I wish to release?"*

  *"What clarity do I seek?"*

  *"How do I want to feel when I wake up tomorrow?"*

- Create a peaceful environment soft music, candlelight, essential oils, or a clean journal nearby.

**Fasting Day – The Sacred Pause**

During your fast, you will refrain from solid food while remaining nourished through hydration and spiritual connection.

Drink throughout the day:

- Filtered water or spring water
- Lemon water or cucumber-infused water
- Herbal teas (peppermint, chamomile, nettle, ginger
- Coconut water (natural, unsweetened)

**Spiritual Practices:**

- Begin your day with prayer or affirmation.
  "I am supported. I am clear. I am connected."

- Sit in meditation call to your Guardian Angel even if just for 10 minutes.
- Practice breathwork to move stagnant energy.
- Spend time in nature, silence, or gentle movement like yin yoga.
- Observe the feeling of hunger as a sacred teacher, not an enemy. Ask what it reveals.

If at any time you feel weak, dizzy, or overly emotional, listen to your body. It is okay to rest, modify, or gently break your fast with fruit or broth.

**Breaking the Fast –with loving kindness**

How you break your fast is just as important as the fast itself. Go slowly and treat your body with gratitude.

First Foods (light and hydrating):

- Watermelon, golden kiwi, papaya, or fresh orange slices
- Light herbal tea or warm water with a pinch of sea salt

Follow with:

- Fresh vegetable broth or steamed vegetables
- Soft cooked grains like millet, brown rice, or quinoa

Avoid heavy, fried, or overly complex meals for the rest of the day. Let your system reawaken gently.

**After the Fast – Integration and Reflection**

- Journal about your experience:

*What did I notice? What emotions came up? What felt uneasy? What felt beautiful?*

- Practice gratitude to your Guardian Angel for balancing cleansing your body and your spirit.
- If it feels right, enjoy a salt bath or grounding foot soak to reconnect.

A plant-based, whole foods diet after fasting continues the feeling of clarity, lightness, and spiritual connection.

These foods carry the life force of the Earth and allow the body to function with greater ease, reducing fatigue and enhancing energy flow.

### Final Thoughts: Fasting as Spiritual Devotion

Fasting is not a test of strength it is a tender surrender.

It is not about proving anything to the world it is about reconnecting with the part of you that is already whole. The part that remembers the divine blueprint within.

When fasting is approached as a spiritual practice, it becomes a form of prayer. An offering. A quiet act of devotion.

May your fast, however simple, be a return to your inner light.

May it cleanse more than the body may it cleanse doubt, fear, stagnation.

May you emerge with clarity, grace and the quiet joy of spiritual alignment.

## *A Final Reflection: Reclaiming Your Power*

Take a moment to pause. Breathe deeply. Reflect on the sacredness of your existence.

You are here for more than just survival you are here to thrive, create, love and embody your divine light.

- ❖ Your body is your temple cherish it.
- ❖ Your mind is your instrument expand it.
- ❖ Your emotions are your compass honour them.
- ❖ Your spirit is eternal embrace it.

Step outside take off your shoes socks feel the earth beneath your feet, let the sun kiss your skin, feel the wind flow through your hair. Know that you are held by the universe, guided by unseen forces, connected to all that is creation. You have one precious life one radiant opportunity to walk with grace, to shine as the light bearer you were born to be. Open your mind to the endless possibility and awaken, the time is now.

## *Living with Heightened Senses – A Spiritual Perception*

Each of us carries the gift of divine perception. Imagine invisible sensors extending from the top of your head, the tips of your fingers, radiating outward in every direction, 360 degrees of awareness

Every sense, smell, taste, sight, touch heightened. And beyond those, a deeper inner knowing awakens: an intuitive awareness of the living spirit that pulses through all things. To live like this is to walk between worlds. To thrive in this world learning to be grounded in the present moment. Is the only reality.

Yes it is wonderful to float away into higher realms have chat with your loved one in spirit that you yearn to hold However you have to live in both worlds to survive

Our spiritual senses often called the Clairs are channels through which we receive higher wisdom:

Clairvoyance – Clear seeing: visions, mental images and prophetic dreams

Clairaudience – Clear hearing: inner voices, whispers, sounds carrying subtle truths

Clairsentience – Clear feeling: emotional and energetic awareness that runs deeper than words

Claircognizance – Clear knowing: sudden insights that need no explanation

Clairgustance – Clear tasting: flavours tied to spirit or memory

Clairalience – Clear smelling: scents with no physical source, acting as spiritual messengers

## *Living with My Sensitivity*

I was born with heightened senses and for much of my life, I didn't know how to manage them. Every sound, every scent, every passing emotion from others, everything entered me deeply. It wasn't just that I noticed the world. I felt it. Intensely. Constantly.

Bright lights overwhelmed me. Loud places drained me. People's moods soaked into my skin like rain. I could sense unspoken thoughts, tensions in the air, grief behind smiles. Sometimes, it was so much I wanted to disappear, curl up and hide from the noise of everything.

For a many years I would question my Guardian Angel Mena, as I thought something was wrong with me. Slowly, I began trust, accept to understand: this wasn't a curse. It was a calling.

Learning control wasn't about shutting down. It was about grounding, breathing and choosing when to open and when to shield. Like tending a sacred fire, I had to learn how to hold my sensitivity with respect, so it could warm and guide instead of burn me out.

Some days I still feel everything at once. Now, I carry tools of stillness, nature, water, breath, silence. I no longer run from my sensitivity. I walk with it, gently.

## *A True Story: The Kitchen Girls heightened Sensitivity*

A young Chinese woman came to me for therapeutic touch. She told me. I would understand her as she could see an angel beside me.

Her family had a small takeaway kitchen where she worked. To her family, she was quiet, kind and diligent yet, within her, something extraordinary stirred.

She could feel the energy of the chickens long after their bodies were prepared for cooking. She heard them, not with her ears, but with the inner hearing of the soul. Their faint chatter lingered in the air: soft clucks of confusion and sadness, even after their heads were removed their spirits didn't leave right away.

She understood that their energy, their life-force, stayed within their bodies for a time. And so, she honoured them. Every time she prepared them, she whispered thank you, offering silent gratitude for their sacrifice. In her hands, food became ceremony. Reverence. A quiet act of gratitude and love

## *My Story: Scent as a Bridge Between Worlds*

Whenever I need help with anything related to building or repairs,

I call to my Dad in spirit he comes with a smell cigarette smoke. It appears out of nowhere. There's no open window, no one smoking nearby. Yet the smell is clear, immediate and familiar. I welcome Dad..

He was a builder who could fix anything. That scent is his signature. A quiet way of saying, I'm here. His presence in those moments is undeniable, practical and deeply comforting, just as he was in life.

Each of my loved ones in spirit have their own distinct scent. It's how they reach me. How they remind me that they're near.

My mother's love arrives in the soft fragrance of Lily of the Valley. It was her favourite in life and it still surrounds me now in moments of vulnerability and grace.

My sister carries the aroma of merlot with a faint trace of cigarette smoke. Her presence feels like late-night talks and shared secrets, wrapped in laughter.

My brother's energy enters with the warm scent of oak pipe tobacco. It's grounding, familiar and protective, like the steady strength he once offered me.

These are not coincidences. They are signs. Gentle, sacred reminders that love does not end. For those who are open to them, signs are everywhere. A fleeting scent. A song that plays at the perfect moment. A whisper that doesn't come through the ears, but is felt through the heart.

As you read this, pause. Take a deep breath. Feel the air move through you. Let it remind you of something sacred.

You are not here only to survive. You are here to feel. To awaken. To remember you are held in unconditional love.

Step outside. Let your bare feet touch the earth. Feel the sun kiss your skin. Let the wind move through your hair.

Your heartbeat is in rhythm with the Earth itself. You are alive in divine spirit and unconditional love. You are never alone.

The veil between the worlds are thinning our loved ones in spirit step forward when you include them in daily activities talk to them as you did when they were with you. Stay grounded, authentic be the best version of you.

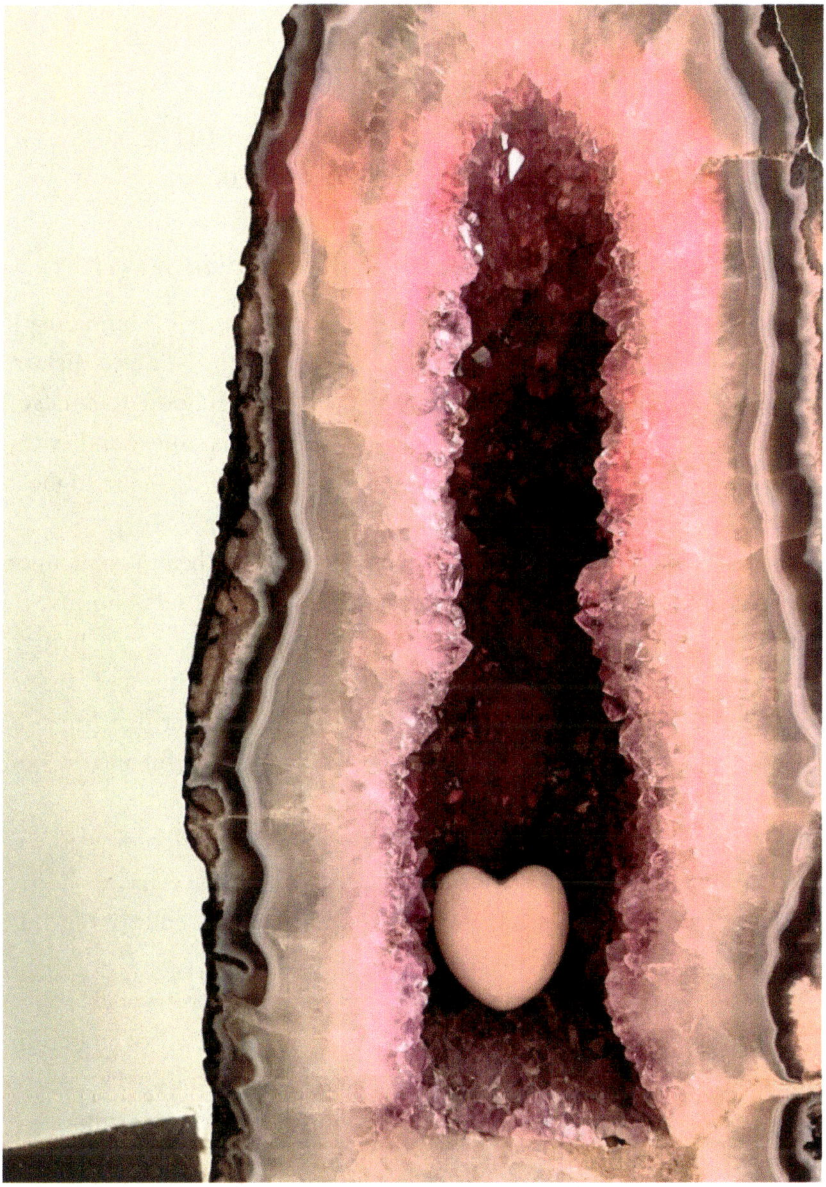

*Photograph of my Amethyst Goddess Geode*

CHAPTER 10

# Transformational Stories and Channelled Meditations

## *Developing a bond with Your Guardian Angel*

Awakening to the Divine Spirit is not just a possibility it is humanity's destiny. We are here to co-create Heaven on Earth. Not as a distant dream as a living reality that unfolds the moment we choose to believe. When we open our hearts with gratitude, loving-kindness and faith, we align with the sacred flow of creation and step into our highest purpose.

I have walked this path, facing financial struggles, health challenges and the demands of raising a family while being self-employed. Through it all, my Guardian Angel, Mena, has been my bridge messenger to the Creator a source of wisdom, healing and divine support. This same bridge is available to you. Your Guardian Angel is always with you, ready to guide you toward s a meaningful and deeper connection to inner peace contentment and purpose.

One of the most powerful ways to awaken this connection is through the vibration of your own voice. Your voice has a sacred frequency and becomes a transmitter, carrying the energy of your soul's intention into the universe.

The spoken word holds immense power and when you speak divine truth, your entire being responds at the deepest level of unconditional love. This is why I encourage you to record these channelled meditations in your own voice because hearing your own vibration amplifies the energy, allowing the wisdom to resonate within you on a profound level.

As you listen to your own sound, words infused with love, healing and intention, you activate the higher frequencies within you. Your voice has the power to awaken your soul. It is a direct key to transformation, guiding you into alignment with the divine.

You are not alone. Heaven or Nirvana, is not a place we go when we pass over it is here, now within every cell of our being. It exists all around us and within us, waiting to be realised.

Nirvana is a state of being we create through unconditional love, trust and gratitude. The time to awaken is now.

## *JP's Case Study: A Journey of Awakening*

When JP first came to me for physical therapy, she was a highly stressed professional woman seeking relief for her tense, overworked body. Yet, from the very first session, it was clear that her journey would involve much more than physical healing.

As she lay face down on the couch, surrendering to the therapeutic process, a profound presence filled the room. Her Guardian Angel appeared, radiating a luminous energy and with them stood the loving spirits of her Mother, Grandmother, Aunt and Uncle. Their unwavering love wrapped around her like a protective embrace, so powerful that it moved me to tears, tears she could not see. At that moment, I knew that our work together would reach far beyond muscles and fascia; it would touch the very core of her being.

JP carried the weight of a lifetime's worth of stress, but beneath that, there were deeper layers, unresolved karmic patterns, emotional wounds infused into her energy field and higher chakras blocked by years of disconnection from her true self. Despite her outward success, a spiritual numbness lingered, preventing her from fully embracing her soul's path.

What unfolded over the course of our sessions was nothing short of transformational, a journey not only of healing but of awakening.

During our treatments, completely guided by my Guardian Angel and JPs I felt a loving connection with the Christ's consciousness. Her family in spirit rejoiced at the possibility of her awakening. However, when I asked her Guardian Angel if I could share this spiritual connection, the answer was clear: she was not ready. It was a time for nurturing, not revelation.

Over the years, I supported JP with therapeutic massage and healing modalities designed to gently release old karmic patterns and invite acceptance and forgiveness into her life. Each session became a sacred space where divine love flowed.

My hands worked on her physical body, while my sacred heart held space for her spiritual and emotional release.

There were many profound moments the sound of chanting, singing holy men and women sometimes, Christian soldiers would enter the room during our sessions, their energy deeply reverent. I incorporated various healing modalities always instructed by my Guardian Angel.

- Crystal Grids: Using kyanite to align her chakras and clear quartz to uplift and purify her energy field, helping her reconnect with her divine essence.
- Galactic and Sacred Heart Healing: Connecting her with Christ Consciousness and divine feminine energies such as Quan Yin (the goddess of mercy and unconditional love), Hathor (the Egyptian goddess of joy and nurturing) and Bastet (who brings protection, empowerment and grounding).
- Karmic Release: Guided by Archangels Metatron and Zadkiel, Tibetan monks and ancient deities, JP began to let go of burdens she had carried for lifetimes. She learned to forgive herself and others, untangling the threads of pain embedded through her life.

One day, during a particularly powerful session, JP's father appeared alongside her family in spirit. I sought guidance from my Guardian Angel and the answer was a resounding "yes," it was time to share his messages of love and healing. Her father spoke of their life together and the struggles they endured after her mother's passing.

With sincere gratitude, he thanked JP for stepping up to care for her younger brother and for creating moments of connection and joy, such as their walks with the family dog.

His words carried profound healing. He urged her to release the guilt she had carried for so long and to trust in the purity of her soul, as he and her entire family in spirit did. Together they encouraged her to embrace her divine calling as a lightworker, assuring her that her compassion and strength made her uniquely suited to guide others toward healing.

Overwhelmed yet deeply moved, JP gradually opened her heart to this path.

Through acceptance, forgiveness and a newfound connection to divine spirit, she overcame significant health challenges, including terminal illness and rediscovered her universal spiritual self.

Currently she dedicates her life to supporting others as a trustee for a holistic charity, embodying the compassionate loving-kindness that transformed her own life. JP's journey is a testament to the power of divine love and the healing that comes from releasing karmic patterns, embracing forgiveness and opening one's heart to spiritual awakening. It reminds us that healing is not merely physical, it is a profound reunion with our true selves, where unconditional love and compassion illuminate the path forward.

## *A Journey of Profound Healing and Rebirth*

When GB first came to me for treatment, I had no idea which guides would come through. As always, I began by invoking my Guardian Angel, as described in previous chapters.

Her partner wheeled her into the room, wrapped tightly in a fleece, her body trembling despite the warmth of summer. The chill that gripped her was more than physical, it came from deep within, a coldness that no amount of heat could touch. It was as though years of pain, exhaustion and unspoken sorrow had settled into her very bones. Her skin was pale, her energy fragile and yet, in her eyes, there was a flicker of quiet determination.

With great care, I helped her onto the couch. She curled into herself, cocooned in the fleece, seeking warmth that no blanket alone could provide. As the session began, I placed my hands on her, calling upon the angels to send forth healing. In those moments, I became a channel for divine energy. GB would often shake as the energy intensified, her body responding to the unseen forces working through her.

Her treatments were a blend of different healing modalities, guided by the divine forces that came forward each time. They included:

- Quartz Crystal Grids – Aligning and amplifying her energy.
- Karma Release with Egyptian Goddesses- Connecting with Sekhmet (the warrior goddess and healer), Isis (symbol of maternal love and wisdom) Hathor and Bastet to access ancient wisdom and restore balance.
- Galactic and Sacred Heart Healing – Linking her to Christ Consciousness and the divine feminine energy of
- Angelic Healing – Calling upon higher realms to infuse her with divine love and renewal.
- Massage and Aromatherapy – Releasing stored trauma and allowing energy to flow more freely.

This treatment was truly incredible, miraculous even, but it did not happen overnight. GB had a lot emotional and physical stuff to work through. The Crystal Kingdom picked up an immense energy and to my amazement, flew around the treatment room. My skin tingled with awe, excitement and deep appreciation for the trust and love that filled the space. I felt humbled to have this opportunity to work with the Masters, witnessing the raw power of divine intervention unfold before me.

During one session, I sought guidance on how much I could reveal to GB and the answer was clear: nothing. She was in the process of being reborn, destined to receive a new body and live a life of joy, creativity and love.

Each treatment was unique. We chanted together, as GB embraced the process, shifting her mindset from feeling unwell to affirming her strength and vitality:

"I am a strong, healthy woman. I am free. I love life."

As her healing progressed, GB began to forgive herself and others, releasing the shadows of her past.

One profound session marked her rebirth, her physical form vibrated intensely, shaking as her energy systems and chakras aligned. It was as if she became a snake, shedding her skin to reveal a vibrant new self. I watched in awe, my heart swelling with gratitude for the divine forces at work.

Today, GB meditates regularly, dances, chants and works within her community to spread joy and harmony. She has embraced her multi-dimensional nature, radiating love in all she does.

Her transformation is a powerful reminder of the divine potential within each of us to heal and thrive.

## *Making Space for Meditations and Prayers*

There was a time when the idea of change filled me with unease a shifting current I longed to control or outrun. But life, in its quiet wisdom, kept inviting me to let go. It was only through the simple, sacred practice of daily meditation that I began to listen. Even a few minutes each day opened a doorway to peace I didn't know was possible.

Meditation became a homecoming a return not to who I was yesterday, but to who I am becoming, moment by moment. It taught me that change is not something to fear or fix, but something to welcome with an open heart. Each breath, each silent pause, became an opportunity to soften, to trust, to realign with the deeper rhythm of life itself.

Practice is not about doing it perfectly. It's about showing up again and again with presence and devotion. Some days, the mind will settle like a lake at dawn; other days, it will toss and turn like a restless sea. Both are part of the path. Both are sacred.

There is no perfect time to meditate, only the one that allows you to meet yourself where you are. For some, the early morning offers a fresh, quiet beginning; for others, the evening brings a chance to reflect, release, and realign.

***What matters is not the hour, but the heart with which we come.***

Through the practice of loving-kindness, we plant seeds of self-compassion that blossom over time. Each breath dissolves old resistance, creating space for authentic healing and transformation. In this sacred stillness, we invite divine guidance to flow freely clearing ancient wounds, illuminating our highest path, and anchoring us more fully in the present moment.

Consistency is the gentle key to profound change. Every time we return to our practice, no matter how imperfectly, we deepen our connection to inner peace. Meditation becomes more than a ritual; it becomes a way of life a steady companion through the ever-changing seasons of our soul.

In the silence of meditation, fear loses its grip. Doubt softens. The mind, once scattered and hurried, learns the gentle art of surrender. Over time, we move through life with greater clarity, resilience, and love, learning to greet each new moment with open arms.

As we cultivate stillness within, the brain responds by releasing soothing endorphins such as serotonin and dopamine, encouraging us into states of relaxation, receptivity, and profound well-being. In this open, tender space, we become vessels for loving-kindness able to hear the nurturing whispers of our soul, feel the presence of our Guardian Angels, and connect with the vast wisdom of our Higher intelligence

Through the simple, sacred act of meditation, we transcend the illusion of separation. We realise that healing within radiates outward, touching every life we meet. As we awaken to the divine love within us, we become carriers of light, peace, and compassion for the world.

Let us walk this path together heart to heart, spirit to spirit embracing meditation not as an occasional retreat, but as a daily devotion to our highest selves and to the healing of all beings. In stillness, in breath, in love, we find our way home

## *Channelled Meditations: A Gateway to the Divine*

The meditations you will find here are not written from thought alone, nor crafted as mere exercises in relaxation.

They are living streams of light pure, channelled transmissions of love and wisdom, gifted to me by my beloved Guardian Angel, Mena.

Each meditation carries the sacred breath of grounding, healing, and ascension, a gentle pathway leading you home to your Higher Self and to the celestial companions who have always walked beside you.

These sacred offerings are tenderly held and protected, their authenticity preserved as an act of devotion to the divine.

I invite you, with an open heart, to record them in your own voice, allowing their energy to weave more deeply into the fabric of your being. In this way, you may strengthen your sacred bond with your Guardian Angel, a radiant messenger of God's eternal love.

In a world woven with noise and forgetting, these meditations create a sanctuary a soft place where the soul may rest, expand, and remember its original light.

They are infused with the frequency of unconditional love, carrying you beyond the veils of the mind, into the vast, boundless presence that has always lived within your heart.

As you journey through these sacred waters, may you find solace for your spirit, clarity for your path, and the sweet remembrance that you have never walked alone.

May each breath, each word, each moment bring you closer to the divine embrace that is your truest home.

## *Awakening the Divine Within - Balance and Align the Chakras*

Your chakras are the sacred gateways between your physical body and the spiritual realm, each one a radiant vortex of energy connecting you to your highest self, the Earth and the divine.

When in harmony they form a bridge between heaven and earth, allowing divine energy to flow freely, bringing balance, clarity and inner peace.

This meditation is a sacred journey of renewal, a reunion with your authentic true essence. As you move through each chakra, you will release stagnant energy, awaken your divine potential and realign with the infinite love of the universe. With the guidance of your Guardian Angel and the celestial presence of Archangel Michael, you will be supported, protected and held in the embrace of divine light.

Before beginning, take a moment to create a peaceful and undisturbed space. Set an intention for your practice, knowing that this meditation is a gift to yourself, a moment of healing, empowerment and connection to the divine forces that walk beside you.

Now, take a deep breath, surrender to the journey and allow the sacred light within you to shine.

**[Important Note: If self- recording ensures not listen to this meditation while driving or operating machinery]**

**Preparation**

Follow steps 1 and 2 in chapter 1. Create a sacred space where you feel safe, undisturbed and fully present. Light a candle, burn incense, or surround yourself with crystals if you feel called to do so.

If you feel guided, record this meditation in your own voice for a more personal connection, as your voice carries the resonance of your soul and Guardian Angel.

Sit upright in a dignified pose or in front of your altar. Close your eyes and take a deep breath. Place your hands over your heart and affirm:

"I AM going to balance and ground my energy. I call upon my Guardian Angel and the divine beings of light to guide me in this sacred practice."

Call upon Archangel Michael, asking for his golden dome of protection to surround, align with your higher purpose.

Begin with five deep breaths. Inhale deeply, drawing in divine light. Exhale slowly, letting go of anything that is not conducive to my health and well- being releasing tension, fear and all that no longer serves you.

As your breathing becomes soft and natural, allow yourself to settle into a state of deep peace and presence.

## *Chakra Balancing Meditation*

***© Marguerite Davies 2000***

Imagine yourself seated beneath a magnificent ancient oak tree. Its strong, wise branches stretch toward the heavens, while its deep roots ground firmly into the earth. Feel the warm sunlight touching your head, shoulders and heart, soothing and comforting.

Now, picture your feet merging with the roots of the tree, extending deep into the embrace of Mother Earth Gaia. With every breath, feel a profound sense of stability, protection and connection to the nurturing energy of the earth.

**Crown Chakra (Top of Head)**

Visualise a radiant funnel of violet, gold and pure white light extending infinitely upward, connecting you to divine consciousness. Feel this celestial energy pouring down, filling you with wisdom, peace and a deep sense of unity with the Creator.

**Third Eye Chakra (Between Eyebrows)**

See a swirling vortex of deep indigo and shimmering gold gently opening. Feel your intuition expanding, your inner wisdom awakening and a deep knowing settling into your being.

**Throat Chakra (Throat)**

Imagine a serene misty blue light expanding from your throat, clearing any blocks. Speak your divine truth with love and clarity, allowing your voice to be a vessel of wisdom and healing.

**Heart Chakra (Centre of Chest)**

Picture soft hues of emerald green and gentle pink swirling in your heart centre. If any old wounds or grief arise, embrace them with compassion. Visualise golden light pouring into the four chambers of your heart, dissolving pain and filling you with unconditional love.

**Solar Plexus Chakra (Below the Stomach)**

See a radiant golden sun glowing in your core, expanding outward with warmth and strength. Allow any feelings of insecurity or doubt to dissolve as this golden light fills you with courage and empowerment.

**Sacral Chakra (Below the Navel)**

Imagine a vibrant orange light swirling joyfully, unlocking your creative flow and sensual energy. Feel passion, inspiration and deep emotional connection awakening within you.

### Root Chakra (Base of Spine)

See a rich ruby-red light anchoring you to the earth, connecting you to your ancestors and your inner strength. Feel yourself fully grounded, safe and supported in all areas of your life.

### Connection to the Earth Star Chakra

Now, envision all these colours blending into a radiant rainbow light flowing down through your feet and into the Earth Star Chakra, located six inches below the ground.

Sense this sacred energy connecting you deeply with Mother Gaia. Feel her loving embrace as she nurtures you, restoring balance to your entire being. As her energy flows back upward, it fills each of your chakras, bringing balance, harmony, peace and divine alignment.

Stay here in stillness for as long as you feel called.

### Closing the Meditation

Imagine your Guardian Angel gently touching each chakra with a white feather, harmonising and balancing your energy. Visualise this feather sweeping down your legs and grounding your energy into the Earth Star Chakra.

Take five deep breaths, inhaling divine light and exhaling gently. Wiggle your fingers and toes, slowly bringing awareness back to your body. When ready, open your eyes.

If you feel excess energy, place your hands on the ground and set the intention to release it to Mother Gaia. Sip water to further ground yourself. If inspired, journal any insights, visions, or feelings that arose during your meditation.

### Final Blessing

May this meditation bring you peace, balance and divine alignment. May you walk forward with renewed clarity, strength and love, always connected to the infinite wisdom within.

You are whole. You are radiant. You are divine.

## *Sacred Heart Meditation: A Journey of Divine Grace and Healing*



This meditation holds deep significance, as it was channelled many years ago by Mena, my Guardian Angel.

Meditation is a powerful tool for grounding your energy and bringing you into the present moment. When you invoke your Guardian Angel during this sacred practice, the healing potential is heightened. Guardian Angels are compassionate beings of light, always ready to provide guidance, protection and support. By welcoming your Guardian Angel into this meditative space, you create an opportunity for profound spiritual alignment, gently dissolving blockages and imbalances in their loving presence.

The Sacred Heart Meditation, as channelled through Mena, is a transformative practice designed to reconnect you with your Guardian Angel. It opens a portal to divine love, offering deep healing for emotional wounds and fostering compassion for yourself and others.

Whether practiced daily or during times of need, this meditation connects you with the unconditional love of the Divine, aligning your heart with grace, peace and harmony.

Through the magnificent energy of Grace Elohim enveloping Gaia, this meditation helps release old patterns, mend the heart and unite you with your highest good. It is a deeply personal, authentic and heartwarming experience, a true gift for your spiritual journey.

Allow this sacred practice to guide you on your path of ascension and oneness with Divine love. Guided Sacred Heart Meditation.

### Preparation

- Your healing sanctuary this place where you will not be disturbed.

❖ Sit or lie down with your spine straight, ensuring your body is relaxed.

❖ Close your eyes and take three deep breaths as you breathe outlet go of anything that does not serve your higher good.

## Opening to Divine Grace

❖ Visualise yourself surrounded by a shimmering light, sphere of silver, blue and white, enveloping you in warmth and protection. • Call upon your Guardian Angel, • Invite the sacred beings of Divine Grace to assist you, Mother Mary, Divine feminine presence, nurturing and compassionate. Archangel Chamuel: Angel of love and joy. Archangel Raphael: Angel of healing and restoration. • imagine these beings encircling you, filling your energy field with soft hues of blue, purple, pink, green, gold and silver light.

❖ Imagine the presence of these divine beings radiating love and healing energy connect with this feeling.

If a memory is uncomfortable know your guided by Guardian through divine grace within your being completely safe secure it is time to heal all wounds scares within your being as you connecting with the Sacred Heart

- Picture your heart as a glowing star of divine light.
- Imagine the four chambers of your heart chakra filling with love and healing energy, radiating into your emotional, physical, mental and spiritual bodies.
- Visualise the whole room Illuminating etheric light, become the light.

See yourself standing in the centre of a vibrant tetrahedron star, a kaleidoscope of colours gently floating higher and higher, through the sky and into the vast cosmos. to the healing sanctuary.

In the distance you see a beautiful white and gold temple. Guided by your Guardian Angel.

You arrive at a sanctuary of magenta, pink, purple, gold and silver, a place of pure healing and transformation. Walking through a haze of bright colourful energy and walking towards the steps you are greeted by two silver white angels who direct you to a silver-platinum plinth where you step into pure white gown. Here you are greeted by divine beings of Grace who assist you in healing your 4-body system emotionally physically mentally and spiritually, opening and unifying all aspects of your being.

**Transformative Healing and Integration**

- 7 divine Angels surround you radiating, soothing, nurturing unconditional love, imagine your chakras aligning into a unified column of divine light, merging your personality, soul and monad into harmony.
- Experience this profound activation of the universal chakra pattern, anchoring the Christ consciousness within your being, carefully listen as you hear and feel beautiful sounds resonating from the universal love and light, in your mind say "I am love. I am whole. I am divine grace." 'I am one with God' Embrace the light of Divine Grace bathe, bask in the outpouring of love from the Holy Mother and her divine angels. Allow this light to permeate every cell, molecule and electron of your being, balancing and healing you across all time and space.
- Let go of the past, release all that does not serve you. There is nothing to fix, only love to embrace. imagine yourself, loved ones, all of humanity and Earth healthy, perfect filled with joy, peace, love and harmony You are now one with Gaia, lifting her

into higher realms of divine energy, assisting in humanity's, Gaia initiation and ascension.

- ❖ Visualise yourself and humanity thriving in a new era of divine love, light, unity and grace.

**Gratitude and Grounding:**

- ❖ Slowly bring your awareness back to the present moment. Envision a beam of radiant white light anchoring you to the vastness of your spirit, fostering a deep sense of connection and peace.".
- ❖ Give thanks to all the divine beings who supported you: Mother Mary, Christ Consciousness, Buddha, Archangels Chamuel and Close your eyes and imagine yourself transported into the moon's gentle embrace, orbiting high above the Earth. Envision yourself surrounded by its soft, luminous glow, a peaceful observer of the beautiful world below.

From this celestial vantage, send waves of love and gratitude to all of humanity. Extend your love to Gaia see her flourishing, healthy completely whole, Feel your heart expand as you offer love to all that flies through the skies, swims in the waters and walks upon the land. Finally, send your loving energy to every rock, crystal and mineral, honouring the Earth's ancient foundation.

In this moment, you are one, united with Gaia the moon, stars, planets, galaxy and all of creation. Breathe deeply, knowing that you are part of this vast, interconnected web of life. The living evolving creative consciousness.

Stay for a while ensure your completely grounded take a sip of water

Let us walk together in this truth, embracing meditation as a divine tool for healing, expansion and spiritual growth.

## *The Healing Temple of Atlantis: A Meditation for Self-Discovery and Divine Purpose*



### Introduction

Welcome to this sacred journey to the Healing Temple of Atlantis. Together, we will reconnect with the divine sanctuary within your subconscious, awakening the paradise that already exists within you, your own Garden of Eden, your Heaven on Earth.

Find a comfortable position, either sitting or lying down. If you wish, wrap yourself in a warm blanket to feel safe and cocooned. Gently close your eyes and bring your awareness to your breath. Inhale deeply and exhale slowly. Allow your body to soften, your mind to quiet and your spirit to open.

If thoughts arise, acknowledge them with kindness and let them drift away like waves returning to the ocean. Bring your focus back to your breath, inhaling peace and exhaling all that no longer serves you.

### Relaxation and Grounding

Take a slow, deep breath in and as you exhale, release any tension stored in your body. Repeat this five times, each breath carrying you deeper into a state of peace.

Now, bring your awareness to your toes. Scrunch them tightly for a moment, then release. Feel the relaxation flowing up through your feet and ankles.

Gently squeeze your knees together and let go, releasing any tightness.

Draw your navel inward, noticing any tension in your lower back and hips. As you exhale, let it dissolve.

Clench your hands into fists, then soften your fingers. Lift your shoulders to your ears, then drop them down, releasing any burdens you carry.

Now, bring your attention to your face. Squeeze your eyes shut, tense your jaw, then relax completely. Let your face soften, your forehead smooth, your lip's part slightly as you surrender into ease.

Scan your body with your inner vision. If you find any lingering tension, breathe into that space and on your next exhale, release it completely. Feel yourself growing lighter, calmer, more serene.

### Journey to Atlantis

In your mind's eye, see yourself standing on a pristine white-sand beach. The air is warm with a soft, golden glow. The ocean stretches before you, endlessly calm, its waves whispering gently at the shore. Above you, the sky is a brilliant, endless blue, unbroken and vast.

A sense of deep peace washes over you. The air itself hums with ancient wisdom, inviting you to journey beyond time, beyond memory, to Atlantis, the land of light and healing.

In the distance, a radiant, multi-coloured boat appears, gliding toward you across the water. Ethereal beings of shimmering light stand aboard, their presence exuding warmth, love and welcome. They call to you in a celestial harmony, a song that resonates deep within your soul.

As you step onto the boat, a wave of serenity envelops you. The vessel moves effortlessly over the water, floating as if carried by a gentle, unseen force. You watch the horizon as an island emerges, lush and vibrant, glowing with colours beyond imagination.

The sky above shimmers in hues of pink, gold and blue. The land is alive with crystalline waterfalls, luminous flowers and towering trees that hum with energy. At the heart of the island radiating light, stands the Healing Temple of Atlantis, a golden sphere encasing a brilliant white and gold sanctuary.

### Entering the Temple

As the boat reaches the shore, you step onto the warm white sand greeted by joyful, shimmering beings. Mer-people play in the water, their laughter like the sound of tinkling chimes. They wave, welcoming your home.

A radiant, emerald-green angel approach, extending a hand. As you take it, a wave of gentle energy flows through you, filling you with warmth and love.

With each step toward the temple, a soft, flowing white gown appears around you. It feels weightless yet protective, infused with divine energy.

The air is perfumed with the delicate scents of jasmine, rose and citrus. You pass through gardens of ancient, luminous trees, their leaves whispering forgotten truths. Somewhere deep inside, you remember this place.

At the temple's entrance, two ethereal beings of light guide you up twelve glowing steps. h step feels sacred, cleansing you of all that no longer belongs to your soul's path.

### Receiving Healing in the Sacred Temple

Inside, the temple glows with golden and blue light. A divine, serene presence, a celestial goddess draped in sapphire robes, greets you with a knowing smile. She gestures toward a multi-coloured crystal plinth at the temple's centre.

You lie down, feeling completely at peace, embraced by a deep sense of safety and love. The crystal beneath you hums, aligning with your energy. You set your intention, whether for healing, guidance, or clarity. Trust that whatever you need will come.

Twelve radiant healing angels gather around, their hands hovering above you. Their light flows into you, golden, warm, luminous. It enters your body, filling every cell, every atom, dissolving pain, fear, doubt. Your chakras align, your spirit harmonises and your very essence glows with divine light.

Breathe deeply and surrender. Allow this sacred energy to heal not just your body, but your heart, your past, your soul's journey across lifetimes.

You are whole.

You are loved.

You are divine.

**Returning with Loving Grace**

When the healing is complete, a golden angel approaches, placing a gentle hand over your heart. A warm wave of gratitude fills you, as the angel whispers a sacred truth:

"You are light. You are love. You are infinite."

The Gods and Goddesses of the temple stand before you, blessing you welcoming respecting and acknowledging the God, Goddess standing in front of them. Their presence lingers in your soul as you give thanks and bless them. Feeling energised refreshed. You step back outside, into the glowing gardens of Atlantis.

As you walk toward the beach, you feel lighter, renewed, radiant, connected to the divine valuing the God, Goddess within. Stepping onto the boat once more, you know that this energy, this wisdom, will remain with you always. You have awakened to the co-creator that you are. Stepping into your boat feeling serenity as it sails back across the till calm waters. The white-sand beach where your journey began comes into view.

As your feet touch the sandy beach once more, you bring this healing, this pure love, into your waking life as it rejoices in your spirit.

### Grounding and Closing

Gently, bring your awareness back to the present. Feel the surface beneath you. Wiggle your fingers and toes. Rotate your ankles. Stretch your arms above your head and take a deep breath in and out.

Imagine a beam of white light flowing from the base of your spine into the earth, grounding you in strength, balance and grace.

When you feel ready, slowly open your eyes. Take a sip of water, feeling the healing energy settle within you. Carry this peace, this divine connection, with you throughout your day. love peace and blessings,

*Marguerite*

## *Lions Gate: A Sacred Time for Light Bearers*

Every year on August 8th, at 8:00 a.m. and 8:00 p.m., a powerful surge of light codes is transmitted to humanity through the Lions Gate portal. This is an extraordinary moment for light bearers, as the Sirian Elders guardians of higher wisdom support humanity's awakening, ascension and spiritual evolution. They honour and respect all those who work with the light, recognising the dedication it takes to uplift consciousness and anchor divine frequencies on Earth.

The Lions Gate portal is a sacred opening in the celestial realms, a time when the flow of cosmic energy is intensified, offering us an opportunity to align with higher wisdom, divine healing and the infinite light of our soul's purpose. Each year, as this portal reaches its peak, we are bathed in the radiant energy of Sirius, the "Spiritual Sun" a celestial beacon that illuminates our path of transformation, awakening and ascension.

During this time of deep spiritual activation, the veil between worlds is at its thinnest, allowing us to receive divine messages, heightened intuition and profound guidance from our Higher Selves and Guardian Angels.

The number eight, with its infinite looping shape, symbolises the endless flow of divine energy, the eternal dance of creation and renewal and the limitless possibilities available to us in this moment.

As Sirius' high-frequency light pours into Gaia, it awakens dormant light codes within us, igniting our divine potential and guiding us into deeper self-discovery and soul remembrance. This cosmic influx of energy is an invitation to release old limitations, embrace healing and step into greater clarity, balance and purpose.

The Sirian energy has long been intertwined with Earth's evolution, carrying the wisdom of ancient civilizations and the harmonic blueprint of the universe.

It is a force of profound love and transformation, offering guidance, healing and ascension to all who attune to its frequency.

This meditation is a sacred invitation to step into the cosmic flow, align with the wisdom of the stars and receive the blessings of the higher realms. As you embark on this journey, may your heart open fully to the divine light within you and may you walk forward with grace, love and the infinite power of your soul's truth.

## *Journey with Your Guardian Angel – A Meditation*

**Channelled by Marguerite Davies,1982**

Your Guardian Angel is a divine being who has walked beside you through every incarnation. Before your very first breath, they knew your soul, your essence, your purpose. They have loved you through lifetimes, held space for your growth, and whispered encouragement in your moments of doubt. Would you like to meet them now, to feel their unique vibrational frequency and experience their presence as a loving, guiding light?

Your Guardian Angel knows you intimately. Understanding your heart, essence, your sensitivities, your struggles and your gifts.

Guiding not with judgement, but with absolute love. Supporting you attune to what is right for you in this moment, not the past, not the future, but now. Through this meditation, you will gently open to Its presence. You may sense, colour, a fragrance, a gentle tingling, or even a quiet word inside your heart. However they appear, let it be a reminder of their constant care. They are a mirror of the divine, sent by God to walk with you.

To begin, find a comfortable position. If sitting, make sure your back is supported. If you are lying down, place a cushion under your knees. Wrap yourself in a soft blanket if needed. Have a glass of water nearby and a notebook ready to capture any reflections afterward.

Now, close your eyes and take five slow, deep breaths, inhaling deeply through your nose and gently exhaling through your mouth.

Let each breath ground you further, quieting your thoughts and anchoring you in the now.

Picture your feet becoming the roots of a great ancient tree extending deep into the Earth, flowing through soil, stone and crystal, finally reaching the glowing heart of Gaia herself. Her core glows like a radiant blue diamond, pulsing with life. Feel your roots wrap gently around it. This is your anchor, your source, your connection to the sacred Earth. Gaia is not just the ground beneath you; she is a living, sentient being.

Feel her strength rising through your feet moving up through your legs and hips, forming the trunk of your tree, solid, stable and strong. Your upper body becomes the branches, stretching wide, covered in leaves of every shade of green. Above you, the golden sun shines down through the canopy, warming your skin, energising your cells, and filling you with light. You are a part of her. The Earth breathes, and you breathe with her.

Bring your awareness now to your physical body. Notice the space around your limbs, the weight of your head, the rhythm of your breath. If there is tension, breathe into that space and let it gently release. Expand your awareness beyond your body, feel the energy in the room. You may hear distant sounds the rustle of trees outside, the hum of a heater, birdsong in the air. Let it all become part of your sacred space.

Imagine now a golden dome of light descending gently around you, placed by Archangel Michael. This is a shield of divine protection, safety and peace. Inside this dome, you are held in sacred stillness. And here, within this space, your Guardian Angel begins to make themselves known.

Imagine them standing behind you now. Feel the warmth radiating from their presence. Perhaps you sense the softness of wings gently enveloping you, like a loving embrace.

You might see a glow, hear a name, or simply feel an overwhelming sense of calm. Silently ask: "What is your name?" and listen not just with your ears, but with your heart. Allow their light to flow into your being, bringing peace, healing and deep remembrance.

Now see yourself walking with them along a quiet country lane. The sun is shining, birds sing from the hedgerows, and a gentle breeze carries the scent of honeysuckle and wild herbs. You feel completely safe, completely held. Your Guardian Angel walks beside you, step for step. In the distance, you hear the sound of rushing water, a soft, melodic cascade. You follow it together, and soon you reach a beautiful waterfall tumbling over smooth stone into a crystal-clear pool below.

Step beneath the waterfall. Let the cool, sparkling water pour over you. Feel it cleansing your energy field, washing away everything that no longer serves you. This is a sacred baptism a purification of body and soul. The water carries away any heaviness, renewing your spirit. You feel lighter, clearer, and whole.

Step out now into the sunlight and lie down on a soft bed of mossy grass. The earth supports you fully. The sun warms your skin, drying you with golden light. You feel the moss beneath your fingertips cool, fresh, ancient. Your Guardian Angel lies beside you, Its presence pulsing with warmth nurturing and serenity. In this moment, basking in the sun's radiance, you feel a powerful, unbreakable connection between spirit and matter between your soul and the Gaia. You are the meeting point of heaven and Earth. The divine and the physical merge within you.

Listen to the song of nature: birds calling from the trees, the rhythmic flow of the waterfall, the whisper of leaves moving in time with your breath. Everything is alive, vibrating with love. Open your heart to the presence of your Guardian Angel.

Their energy gently weaves into yours. At this point, you may hear a sound a soft inner tone, feel a tingling vibration, or simply know that they are here. Let this moment imprint on your soul.

As your journey gently comes to a close, begin to walk back along the path, hand in hand with your Guardian Angel.

The fields are alive with wildflowers, and the woods shimmer with emerald light. With each step, you feel refreshed, realigned, and deeply supported. You carry this connection within you it is part of you.

Pause and thank your Guardian Angel for their love, their guidance, and their eternal companionship. Know that they are always near, ready to guide, comfort, and uplift you whenever you call.

Now, slowly bring your awareness back into your body. Gently move your fingers and toes. Take a few deeper breaths. When you are ready, open your eyes. Sip your water. Take a quiet moment to reflect, and if you feel called, write or sketch your experience. There is no right or wrong whatever you felt or saw is exactly what your soul needed.

This meditation has been brought to you with love and light by Marguerite Davies, Angelic Master and Holistic Therapist. Please do not listen to this recording while operating machinery or driving.

## *Full Moon Lunar Meditation: A Journey of Divine Connection, Balance and Grounding*

Bathe in the luminous glow of the full moon and allow its celestial energy to awaken something deep within you. The moon has long been a source of mystery, wisdom and divine feminine power, a sacred mirror reflecting the ever-changing tides of life.

It whispers to us through the shifting cycles, inviting us to release what no longer serves us and embrace the light of renewal.

Tonight, beneath the moon's gentle radiance, you are called to reconnect, with yourself, with the Earth and with the infinite universe that flows through every breath. The full moon is not only a time of illumination but of deep reflection, a time to honour the journey you have walked and the infinite possibilities still before you.

This meditation is an invitation to step into the moon's embrace, to surrender into its healing energy and to align with the divine rhythm that guides all of creation. Let your heart open, your spirit soften and your soul dance in the moonlight as you welcome the sacred energies of the Universe.

Take a deep breath and allow yourself to be fully present. The moon is watching over you. You are held. You are loved. You are divine.

### Creating Your Sacred Space

Choose a peaceful and quiet place where you feel safe and nurtured. If possible, sit outdoors beneath the full moon, allowing its radiant light to touch your skin. If you are indoors, sit near a window or place a moonstone, selenite, or a bowl of water nearby to invite the moon's energy into your space.

Sit comfortably, either on the ground or in a chair, ensuring your feet connect with the Earth. Rest your hands gently in your lap, palms open, ready to receive the Universe's loving energy.

Close your eyes and take a slow, deep breath in. Feel the cool night air filling your lungs, then exhale softly, releasing all tension.

## Welcoming the Moon's Inspiration

As you settle into the moment, allow the moonbeams to caress your senses, their gentle light sparking your imagination and filling you with uplifting, divine inspiration. Invite the moon fairies to join your sacred space.

In your mind's eye, see them shimmering and dancing, their energy playful and light. You might feel your body naturally begin to sway or move, as though you are dancing in harmony with them. If it feels right, chant softly:

"Luna moon, I am one with you.

Our energy is one, pure and true."

Close your eyes and imagine yourself transported into the moon's gentle embrace, orbiting high above the Earth. Envision yourself surrounded by its soft, luminous glow, a peaceful observer of the beautiful world below.

From this celestial vantage, send waves of love and gratitude to all of humanity. Extend your love to all that is green: every tree, blade of grass, flower and vine. Feel your heart expand as you offer love to all that flies through the skies, swims in the waters and walks upon the land. Finally, send your loving energy to every rock, crystal and mineral, honouring the Earth's ancient foundation.

In this moment, you are united with the moon, the Earth and all of creation. Breathe deeply, knowing that you are part of this vast, interconnected web of life.

## Breathing and Letting Go

Close your eyes and take a deep breath in, slowly filling your lungs with air. Hold it for a moment, then gently release it, feeling any tension leave your body. With each exhale, imagine yourself letting go of stress and distractions.

As you breathe, feel the soft, nurturing light of the full moon surrounding you.

This light is pure and radiant, a reminder of your connection to the celestial cycles and the divine energies that guide you.

### Calling Upon Your Guardian Angels

In your heart, silently invite your Guardian Angel and any loving angelic beings to join you. Feel their presence as a warm, comforting energy surrounding and protecting you.

Say softly in your mind:

"Beautiful Guardian Angel being of love and light, I invite you into this sacred space.

Surround me with your peace and guide me in this meditation.

Help me align with my highest self and bring balance to my mind, body and spirit." Feel their response as the energy of unconditional love washes over you. Know you are safe, supported and deeply loved unconditionally.

### Grounding Your Chakras with the Luna Moon's Energy

Bring your awareness to your body and imagine a beautiful column of moonlight flowing from the full moon above, entering through the crown of your head. This moonlight is gentle and soothing, flowing through each chakra to cleanse ground and balance it:

- Crown Chakra (Top of Head): Radiant white or violet light opens you to divine wisdom and connection.
- Third Eye Chakra (Forehead): Indigo light enhances your intuition and clarity of thought.
- Throat Chakra (Throat): Soft blue light encourages truth, communication and expression.
- Heart Chakra (Chest): Glowing green or pink light fills your heart with love, compassion and acceptance.
- Solar Plexus Chakra (Stomach): Golden light ignites your personal power and confidence.

- Sacral Chakra (Lower Abdomen): Warm orange light fosters creativity and emotional balance.
- Root Chakra (Base of Spine): Deep red-light grounds you in safety and stability.

Allow the lunar moon's energy to align and balance these centres, filling you with peace love and harmony.

**Grounding Into the Earth (Gaia)**

Call to your Guardian Angel and ensure your chakras energy is balanced and grounded.

Let us now, focus on your root chakra. Imagine strong, deep roots growing from the base of your spine and extending down into the Earth. These roots connect you to Gaia, the loving spirit of the planet.

Feel her energy rise through your roots, a nurturing and steady presence grounding you in the here and now. Let her strength fill you with a sense of stability and belonging.

Say silently:

"Thank you, Mother Gaia, for holding me, grounding me and supporting me.

I am one with your energy, balanced and at peace."

**Closing the Meditation**

Take a few more deep breaths, feeling the combined energies of the lunar moon, your angels and the Earth Gaia flowing through you. When you feel ready, gently open your eyes.

Take a moment to reflect on the peace you feel. Know that you are connected to the Universe, supported by loving forces and grounded in the strength of the Earth.

Carry this calm, balanced energy with you as you move forward, embracing the magic of the full lunar moon.

**Final Lunar Blessing**

"May the light of the full moon fill your heart with love.

May you walk in harmony with the cycles of the Universe.

May you always remember that you are divine, radiant and deeply loved."

You are whole. You are radiant. You are one with the Lunar Moon, the Earth Gaia, the stars the universe and the Creator.

[Author Marguerite Davies]

## *New Year's Eve: A Celebration of Release and Renewal*

*© Rita Davies 2000*

New Year's Eve is more than a countdown or a transition from one calendar year to the next. It is a sacred threshold, a powerful moment to pause, reflect and consciously step forward into a new chapter. It is a time of release, shedding the weight of the past and renewal, embracing the limitless possibilities that lie ahead.

The energy of this night is infused with transformation. As one year ends and another begins, the universe offers us a unique opportunity to realign with our highest path.

When setting clear intentions and inviting divine support, we open ourselves to blessings, healing and the wisdom of our Guardian Angel, who walks beside us, guiding our journey.

This ritual is a sacred act of co-creation, a chance to consciously release what no longer serves you and to plant the seeds of new beginnings. It is a time to honour your journey, acknowledge your growth and step forward with clarity, purpose and trust in the divine.

As you prepare to welcome the new year, let this ritual be your moment of stillness and connection. May it guide you in releasing the past with gratitude, embracing the future with hope and stepping forward with the unwavering support of your Guardian Angel. The universe is listening, your heart is open and the path ahead is filled with light.

***What You will Need***

- ❖ A small fireproof bowl or cauldron (or a safe outdoor firepit).
- ❖ Paper and a pen or pencil.
- ❖ A white candle for new beginnings
- ❖ Another candle for releasing the old.
- ❖ Incense or herbs for cleansing (e.g. White sage, rosemary, or frankincense).
- ❖ A small bowl of water and a pinch of salt.
- ❖ Optional: crystals (e.g., clear quartz, amethyst, or moonstone).

**The Ritual**

***Prepare Your Sacred Space***

Choose a quiet, safe space for your ritual. If possible, perform it outdoors to connect with nature or under the stars. Cleanse your space with incense or herbs, wafting the smoke around the area and yourself. Say:

"I cleanse this space of all negativities, creating a sacred place for renewal and transformation."

Arrange your items on a small altar or surface. Light a candle and the incense to set the your intention Call to your Guardian Angel for support.

***Ground Yourself***

Sit comfortably and close your eyes. Take a few deep breaths, feeling your body relax with each exhale. Imagine roots extending from your feet deep into the Earth, grounding you firmly in the present moment.

***Invite Your Guardian Angel***

Place your hands over your heart and call upon your Guardian Angel. Say:

"Beautiful Guardian Angel, I invite you to join me in this sacred space. Surround me with your loving presence. Guide my intuition as I release what no longer serves me and welcome in the blessings of the new year. I open my heart to your wisdom and light."

Feel a gentle, loving energy surrounding you, like a warm embrace or a soft glow. Trust your intuitive self to sense the messages and guidance your Guardian Angel may offer during this ritual.

***Reflect on the Past Year***

Hold the paper and pen. Think about the year that has passed, acknowledging both the joys and the challenges.

Write down anything you wish to release, old habits, fears, regrets, or anything that no longer serves your highest good.

As you write, call to your Guardian Angel, gently guiding your hand helping you recognise what you are ready to let go of. Say silently or aloud:

"With gratitude, I value the lessons of the past year. I release what no longer serves me, making space for new growth and possibilities."

***Burn and Release***

Carefully burn the paper in the fireproof bowl or firepit, watching the flames consume your words. As the smoke rises, imagine your burdens being carried away by the angels.

***Say:***

"As this smoke ascends, I release the past. May it transform into light and wisdom for the path ahead."

Take a moment to feel lighter and freer.

***Set Your Intentions for the New Year***

Light the white candle, a symbol of fresh beginnings and new energy. On a fresh piece of paper, write down your hopes, dreams and intentions for the coming year.

Be specific and heartfelt. If you are seeking a partner, take a moment to reflect on the qualities and personality traits that would complement yours, creating a harmonious and fulfilling connection.

As you write, let your intuitive higher self-guide you. Focus on what feels most important and meaningful. What sparks joy and hope in your heart?

When you are finished, hold the paper in your hands and say:

"I call upon my Guardian Angel for wisdom, renewal and creation. May these intentions grow strong and true, bringing abundance and joy in the year ahead."

Fold the paper gently and place it in a special spot where you can revisit it throughout the year, keeping your intentions alive and aligned with your journey.

### *Blessing and Gratitude*

Sprinkle sea salt into the bowl of water, creating a sacred blessing water. Dip your fingers into the water and anoint your forehead or heart, saying:

"I bless myself with the energy of renewal, balance and peace. May I walk forward with clarity and purpose, guided by my intuition and the love of my Guardian Angel."

Take a moment to thank your Guardian Angel for their loving presence. You may say:

"Thank you, beloved Guardian Angel, for your guidance, protection and light. I walk into the new year with trust in your support and faith in my journey."

### *Closing the Ritual*

Blow out the candles, thanking them for their light and energy. Take a few deep breaths, feeling grounded and at peace. If outdoors, take a moment to gaze at the stars, feeling the infinite possibilities of the new year.

Say "The circle is open but unbroken. May the energy of this night guide me into a year of blessings and positivity. ''So, be it. It, is done''

### *Optional Additions*

- Share the ritual with friends or family, encouraging everyone to participate in their own reflection and intention-setting.
- Incorporate drumming, chanting, or dancing to raise celebratory energy as you welcome the new year.
- Toast to the new year with a favourite drink, offering a portion to the Earth as gratitude.

### *Embracing the New Year with Grace and Purpose*

This ritual is a powerful way to honour the turning of the wheel and step into the new year with clarity, intention and hope. Each step allows you to align with the energy of renewal, supported by your Guardian Angel and your intuitive self.

As you move forward into the new year, carry the wisdom of this sacred practice with you. Let the past rest in gratitude, embrace the present with trust and walk toward the future with an open heart. The universe is ready to meet you where you are, guiding you toward the highest expression of your soul's journey.

May your path be illuminated with love, may your intentions manifest with grace and may the new year bring you abundance, healing and divine blessings.

### *Prayers and Mantras*

As both a Catholic and a universal soul, I hold dear a variety of prayers and mantras that nurture my spiritual journey. Among them are the Our Father, Hail Mary and Glory Be, foundational prayers of my Catholic faith. Alongside these, I also embrace the Great Invocation and the Soul and Monad invocations, inspired by the teachings of Alice Bailey. Together, these prayers deepen my connection to the divine and align me with my higher purpose.

## *Alice Bailey: Soul and Monad Overview*

Alice Bailey's teachings, shared through the Lucis Trust, focus on spiritual growth by connecting with the Soul and realising the Monad, the divine spirit within.

### *The Soul*

The Soul acts as the link between the personality, which includes the mind, emotions and body and the divine spirit. It represents higher consciousness, love and purpose, guiding people toward spiritual awakening and alignment with a higher plan.

- **Key Role:** To connect the personality with divine will and love.

- **Soul Invocation:**
  I am the Soul
  I am the Light Divine
  I am Love
  I am Will
  I am Fixed Design

### *The Monad*

The Monad is the pure divine spark and the source of the Soul. It represents the highest level of spiritual existence and the ultimate connection to the divine.

- **Key Role:** The eternal light that connects each person to the universal source of all life.

- **Monad Invocation:**
  The Light is radiant within me and around me
  The Love of the Divine Self enfolds me
  The Power of the Life Divine lifts me into the Light
  That which is the Divine Self breathes through me and expresses itself through me
  I am that Self.

### *The Great Invocation [original word Men ]*

From the point of Light within the Mind of God
Let Light stream forth into the minds of Humanity.
Let Light descend on Earth.

From the point of Love within the Heart of God
Let Love stream forth into the hearts of Humanity.
May Christ return to Earth.

From the centre where the Will of God is known
Let purpose guide the little wills of Humanity.
The purpose which the Masters know and serve.

From the centre which we call the race of Humanity.
Let the Plan of Love and Light workout,
And may it seal the door where evil dwells.

Let Light and Love and Power restore the Plan on Earth.

As a light bearer, this mantra deeply resonates with my soul. I say it daily, drawing comfort and strength from its sacred words.

My Guardian Angel, Mena, assures me that each time it is recited, I connect with millions of universal light bearers, joining a radiant network of love and healing energy that spans the cosmos.

These words are a beacon, uniting us in purpose and illuminating the path of compassion and divine grace.

### *The Lightworker's Creed: A Sacred Calling*

To walk the path of a Lightworker is to embrace a sacred mission a mission of love, healing, illumination, and service to all living beings. It is a calling felt not in the mind, but deep within the soul a quiet yet unshakable knowing that we are here for something greater than ourselves. We are here not only to awaken to our own divine nature but also to be gentle guides for others as they, too, remember their light.

Each healing we experience, each truth we embody, and each act of compassion we offer ripples outward in ways seen and unseen. Like a stone dropped into still waters, our light travels further than we may ever realise, touching hearts, mending spirits, and inspiring change across time and space.

This creed is more than mere words. It is a living invocation, a sacred affirmation of our soul's purpose. It is a beacon that connects us to the vast, radiant web of Lightworkers across the world and beyond.

My Guardian Angel, Mena, reminds me often that every time we speak these words with true intention, we strengthen this divine network.

Our sacred lights becomes a luminous lighthouse of healing, hope, and transformation across the Earth.

Let this be your daily remembrance of who you truly are. Let it anchor you when the world feels heavy. Let it rekindle your sacred flame when you feel weary. Let it be a love letter to yourself and a vow to the world. For every time you realign with your truth, you offer a healing not only to yourself but to all of humanity.

Stand in your light. Speak your creed. And know that you are never alone on this sacred path.

### *Lightworker's Creed*

I am a Lightworker.
I awoke so that others may awaken.
I learn so that others may also learn.
I transform so that others may transform.
I lighten my load so that others may change theirs.
I learn to see so that others may also see.
I forgave myself so that I may help others to forgive.
I love myself so that I can bring out love in others.
I live to give comfort.
I live to shine loving light unto others.
I live to heal.

I live to give hope.
I live for truth.
I live to love.

— *Author Unknown*

As this chapter concludes, may the stories and meditations shared here serve as a gentle reminder of the boundless love and healing that eternally surrounds and sustains us.

Transformation is not merely about changing who we are; it is a sacred returning a remembering of our true, divine nature.

Each moment of self-acceptance, forgiveness, and loving-kindness aligns us more deeply with our highest destiny: to live as radiant beings of light, whose love and grace uplift not only humanity, but Gaia herself the living, breathing soul of the Earth and the entire Solar System beyond.

To walk in the light is to walk rooted and grounded upon the sacred Earth, to feel the heartbeat of Gaia rising through the soles of our feet, to breathe her life-force into our being. It is to recognise that she is not a distant force, but a sentient, loving companion on our journey, evolving with us, dreaming with us, healing with us.

Know that you are never alone; divine guidance enfolds you in every moment. Your Guardian Angel walks beside you, whispering

encouragement to your spirit, steadying your steps with invisible hands of light. Through loving-kindness, through meditation, through steadfast faith in the goodness of the universe, you hold within you the power to heal, to inspire, and to transform not only your own life, but the lives of all those whose paths cross yours.

Together, through courage, compassion, and a shared vision of unity, we can co-create a future overflowing with joy, harmony, and grace.

One step, one breath, one heartbeat closer to manifesting Heaven on Earth.

***Please awaken and remember.***

Remember that the light you seek has always been within you, waiting patiently for you to turn inward and recognise its brilliance.

As I continue along this sacred path, I do so with an open heart and a curious mind, trusting that the journey itself is the destination. Every experience, every lesson, every soul connection is a stepping stone placed lovingly along the road to ascension.

I invite you to walk this path too to trust in your own inner wisdom, to honour the truth of your authentic self, and to move in harmony with the great divine current that flows through all beings, all worlds, all existence.

Life is not meant to be merely endured; it is meant to be lived fully and tenderly, not in pursuit of unattainable perfection, but in devotion to the beauty of presence, connection, and love.

True fulfilment is found in the simple joys: the touch of a breeze against your skin, the laughter shared with a friend, the silent peace of a moment spent in awe of a sunset.

This is both a physical and spiritual journey a path of natural living, self-healing, and conscious ascension.

It is a way of life that does not strip us of who we are, but roots us more deeply into our sacred essence, connecting us ever more intimately with the pure Divine Love that has always been our truest home.

*tetrahedron star the Human light body*

# Glossary of Meanings

**Angel**

A celestial being often considered a messenger of divine guidance, protection and love. In spiritual traditions, angels are believed to offer support, inspiration and healing, acting as intermediaries between the divine and humanity. Some people experience their presence as intuitive knowing, coincidences, comforting energy, or signs such as repeated numbers or feathers.

**Archangels**

High-ranking angels in various spiritual traditions who act as messengers, protectors and guides between the divine and humanity. Each Archangel is associated with specific qualities, energies and areas of support. For example:

High-ranking angels in various spiritual traditions who act as messengers, protectors and Archangel Michael: Protector and leader, associated with strength, courage and cutting through fear.

- **Archangel Raphael:** Healer of physical, emotional and spiritual wounds, known for guiding health and well-being.
- **Archangel Gabriel:** Messenger and communicator, often connected to inspiration, creativity and clarity.
- **Archangel Metatron:** Keeper of divine records, associated with spiritual transformation and sacred geometry, particularly Metatron's Cube.
- **Archangel Uriel:** The light of wisdom, offering insight, peace and solutions in challenging situations.

**Atmic**

Derived from the Sanskrit word "Atman," meaning "self" or "soul," Atmic refers to the spiritual aspect of the self that connects to universal consciousness and the divine essence.

**Aura**

A subtle, luminous energy field that surrounds a living being. It is often described as an electromagnetic or spiritual force that reflects one's emotions, thoughts and overall well-being. Auras can be perceived as assorted colours, each representing various states of mind, emotions and spiritual vibrations.

**Chakra**

A Sanskrit word meaning "wheel" or "disk," chakras are energy centres in the body that correspond to different physical, emotional and spiritual states. The seven main chakras align along the spine, from the base to the crown of the head.

**Channelled Message**

Guidance received from a higher spiritual source, such as a Guardian Angel, Archangel, ascended master, or light being shared through an intuitive, receptive state..

**Divine Consciousness**

The ultimate state of awareness or intelligence associated with the divine or universal source. It represents a transcendent understanding that embodies unity, love and infinite wisdom, often experienced as a deep connection to all existence and a sense of oneness with higher spiritual truth.

**Divine Grace**

The unconditional love, support, and assistance freely given by a higher power. Seen as a transformative force, it brings healing, guidance, and spiritual upliftment, helping individuals overcome challenges and align with their higher purpose. Associated with compassion, forgiveness, and the presence of the divine.

**Divine Spirit**

The sacred, universal presence seen as the source of life, love and wisdom. Often viewed as a higher power or creative force that transcends the physical world, guiding with unconditional love, compassion, and unity. It may be experienced as intuition, inner peace, or a deep connection to the divine.

**Dis-Ease (Spiritual Meaning)**

A state of imbalance or disharmony within the mind, body, or spirit. It reflects the lack of "ease" caused by unresolved emotions, spiritual disconnection, or energetic blockages. Addressing dis-ease involves healing emotional roots, restoring harmony and reconnecting with one's inner self and divine energy.

**Earth's Energy Grid**

A network of interconnected energetic pathways or ley lines believed to crisscross the planet, linking sacred sites, power points and natural phenomena. Often associated with spiritual and metaphysical traditions, the Earth's energy grid is thought to channel and distribute energy, supporting balance, harmony and vitality for the planet and its inhabitants.

**Earth Star Chakra**

An energy centre located below the feet, often associated with grounding, stability and connection to the Earth's energy. It anchors one's energy field to the physical realm.

**Elementals of Nature**

Spiritual beings or energetic forces associated with the four classical elements: Earth, Water, Air and Fire. These entities, often depicted in folklore and metaphysical traditions, are believed to govern and embody the natural world. Commonly known as gnomes (Earth), undines (Water), sylphs (Air) and salamanders (Fire), they represent the spiritual essence of each element and are said to assist in maintaining the balance of nature. Some traditions also recognise a fifth element, Ether (or Spirit), associated with divine consciousness and the unseen realms.

**Energetic Frequency**

The vibrational resonance of a being or essence, reflecting its consciousness, emotions, or intentions. Higher frequencies align with love and peace; lower ones with fear or negativity.

**Esoteric**

Refers to hidden or deeper spiritual knowledge, typically understood or appreciated by a small group of individuals with advanced understanding or a strong spiritual inclination.

**Family in Spirit**

A group of souls or spiritual beings connected by love, mutual support and shared purpose beyond physical or biological ties. Often regarded as a spiritual family, they may include ancestors, guides, or kindred spirits who provide guidance, comfort and encouragement on one's spiritual journey.

**Feeling Body**

The aspect of an individual that processes and experiences emotions and sensations on a physical and energetic level. It is often seen as the bridge between the mind, body and spirit, helping to navigate emotional awareness, intuition and connection to one's inner world..

**Fifth Plane**

A level of spiritual awareness and existence beyond the physical and astral planes. It is associated with profound love, wisdom and divine understanding.

**Flower of Life**

A geometric pattern composed of multiple evenly spaced, overlapping circles arranged in a hexagonal structure. It is considered a sacred symbol in various spiritual, philosophical and religious traditions, representing the interconnectedness of all life, creation and the universe.

**Gaia**

An ancient Greek name for the personification of Earth, often seen as the "Earth Mother" or living spirit of the planet. Gaia embodies nurturing, life-giving energy and symbolises harmony, balance, and interconnection. She also represents ecological awareness and our responsibility to care for the Earth.

**Galactic Healing**

A spiritual healing practice that draws on cosmic energies to restore balance, clear blockages, and raise vibrational frequency. It connects individuals to universal wisdom and supports intuitive insight and transformation.

**Guardian Angel**

A divine, celestial being messenger to God, assigned to guide, protect and support an individual throughout their life. Guardian Angels offer unconditional love, wisdom and encouragement, helping to navigate challenges, strengthen spiritual connections and align with one's higher purpose. They communicate through intuition, signs and gentle guidance, always respecting free will.

**God**

The supreme being or divine entity, regarded as the creator and sustainer of the universe in various traditions. Often described as all-powerful, all-knowing and ever-present, God is associated with qualities like love, wisdom and justice, inspiring devotion and worship.

**Higher Self**

The divine, intuitive, or spiritual aspect of an individual that transcends the ego and physical existence. It represents one's true essence, offering guidance, wisdom and a deeper connection to universal truth and purpose. The higher self is often seen as the bridge to spiritual enlightenment and inner peace.

**Human Senses**

The physiological abilities that allow humans to perceive and interpret their environment. Traditionally, these include five primary senses: sight, hearing, smell, taste and touch. Expanded models may also include additional senses like balance, temperature, pain and proprioception (awareness of body position). Together, the senses provide a holistic experience of the physical world.

**Indian Ayurvedic Principles**

Core concepts of Ayurveda, an ancient Indian healing system focused on balance in body, mind, and spirit. Based on three doshas Vata, Pitta, and Kapha, it uses diet, lifestyle, herbs, and spiritual practices to support health and healing.

**Golden Ratio**

A mathematical proportion (approximately 1.618) found in nature, art and architecture, where the ratio of two quantities is the same as the ratio of their sum to the larger quantity. Often associated with beauty, harmony and balance, it appears in natural patterns, classical design and sacred geometry.

**Indigo Children**

Spiritually gifted, intuitive, and sensitive children believed to have incarnated with a mission to elevate human consciousness. They often resist rigid systems, show deep empathy, and possess a strong sense of purpose. Many are misunderstood in traditional settings and may also be neurodivergent, reflecting both spiritual and neurological uniqueness.

**Inner knowing**

A deep, intuitive understanding or certainty that arises from within, often described as a "gut feeling." It is independent of external evidence or reasoning and reflects a connection to one's true self, instincts, or universal truth.

**Kabbalah**

An ancient mystical tradition rooted in Judaism, Kabbalah explores the nature of the divine, creation and the spiritual structure of the universe. It provides a framework for understanding life's deeper mysteries and one's connection to the divine.

**Karma**

A Sanskrit term meaning "action" or "deed," karma refers to the spiritual principle of cause and effect, where every action generates a corresponding result. It emphasises the importance of mindfulness and ethical living.

**Kindred Spirit**

A person with whom you feel a deep, natural connection. Kindred spirits often share similar values, beliefs, or experiences, creating a sense of mutual understanding and kinship.

**Language of Light**

A form of spiritual communication expressed through sound, symbols, or vibration. It is believed to carry divine frequencies that activate spiritual awareness and healing at a soul level.

**Metatron's Cube**

A sacred geometric symbol composed of 13 circles interconnected by straight lines. It represents the flow of energy within the universe and is associated with Archangel Metatron. This symbol is used in meditation, healing to balance and harmonise energy.

**Metta**

A Pali word for loving-kindness, benevolence, and unconditional love. Central to Buddhist practice, it reflects selfless compassion for all beings oneself, loved ones, strangers, and even those in conflict transcending attachment, anger, and judgment..

**Mindfulness**

A mental state or practice focused on being fully present and aware in the moment, without judgment. It involves consciously observing thoughts, emotions and surroundings with openness and acceptance. Mindfulness is often used to reduce stress, enhance focus and promote emotional well-being.

**Monad**

A term in spiritual philosophy referring to the indivisible, eternal source of all existence. It represents the purest, most essential form of the soul or spirit that originates from the divine.

**Multi-Dimensional**

Refers to the idea that existence encompasses multiple planes of reality beyond the physical realm. It acknowledges that humans and the universe operate simultaneously on physical, emotional, mental and spiritual levels.

**Neurodivergence**

A term for brain function that differs from the typical, including autism, ADHD, dyslexia, and more. Neurodivergent individuals often have unique sensitivities, perspectives, and gifts. Spiritually, they may carry deep intuition and creativity, contributing to human evolution.

### Orb (Spiritual)

A sphere of energy or light often associated with spiritual presence and significance. Orbs may represent angels, spirit guides, or departed loved ones offering guidance and protection. They are also seen as concentrated forms of divine energy, symbolising unity, healing and higher consciousness. Often perceived visually as glowing orbs of light or appearing in photographs, their colour can hold specific meanings:

- **White/Silver**: Purity and divine presence.
- **Gold**: Enlightenment and wisdom.
- **Green**: Healing and harmony.
- **Blue**: Peace and communication.
- **Pink**: Love and compassion

### Pali

An ancient language that originated in the Indian subcontinent. It is strongly associated with the early texts of **Theravāda Buddhism**, which preserve the teachings of the Buddha. Pali serves as the liturgical language of Theravāda Buddhism and is used in its authorised texts, collectively known as the **Pāli Canon** or **Tipiṭaka** (Three Baskets).

### Sacred Chamber of the Heart

A spiritual space within the heart that serves as a sanctuary for connecting with your soul and divine essence. It is a place of profound peace, unconditional love and spiritual awakening.

### Sacred Geometry

The study of geometric patterns and shapes that are believed to have spiritual, symbolic, or metaphysical significance. Found in nature, art and architecture, these shapes such as the Flower of Life, the Golden Ratio and the Fibonacci sequence are thought to represent the fundamental structure of the universe and the interconnectedness of all things.

**Sixth Sense**

The intuitive ability to perceive beyond the five physical senses (sight, hearing, taste, touch, smell). Associated with heightened awareness, inner knowing, extrasensory perception (ESP), The sixth sense is linked to intuition, spiritual insight and the connection to higher consciousness.

**Soul**

The eternal, divine essence of a person that transcends physical existence. The soul carries the wisdom, experiences and purpose of an individual's journey through lifetimes.

**Soul Star Chakra**

An energy centre located above the crown chakra, often associated with divine guidance, spiritual insight and connection to the soul's purpose. It bridges the individual to higher planes of consciousness.

**Spiritual Ascension**

A journey of personal growth and rising consciousness, marked by healing, inner connection, and awakening. It brings greater peace, purpose, and alignment with one's true self or divine nature.

**Spiritual**

Relating to the intangible aspects of existence, spirituality is the pursuit of connection to something greater than oneself, such as the divine, universal truths, or inner peace.

**Spirit**

The non-physical essence or life force that animates living beings, often considered the core of one's identity or consciousness. In spiritual and philosophical contexts, it is associated with the soul, divine energy, or a higher power, representing the eternal and intangible aspect of existence.

### Spiritual Universal Law

Principles that govern the universe's spiritual and energetic flow, guiding human experience and growth. Laws like Attraction, Karma, and the Law of Three (creation, maintenance, transformation) emphasize harmony, interconnectedness, and alignment with higher truths.

### Vagus Nerve

A major nerve running from the brainstem to the abdomen that influences the parasympathetic nervous system. It is key to regulating stress, emotional balance overall well-being and is often linked to mind-body practices.

### Wholistic

An approach that considers the interconnectedness of mind, body, spirit, and emotions, aiming for balance and well-being by addressing the whole person, not just isolated symptoms.

# Epilogue to 7 Steps to Reconnect with Your Guardian Angel – A Divine Journey

As you reach the final pages of this book, I invite you to take a deep breath and pause for a moment. Feel the stillness around you the gentle presence of something greater. A quiet yet powerful love has always been with you, patiently waiting for you to remember.

This journey has not been about seeking something outside of yourself, but rather about rediscovering what has always been within. At times, life may feel overwhelming, making us question our purpose or feel disconnected from the divine. I understand this feeling, because I have been there too. Yet through every challenge, one truth has remained: you are never alone.

There is a guiding light that walks beside you whether you call it a Guardian Angel, divine intelligence, higher self, or inner wisdom. It is always present, always patient, always waiting for you to turn inward and listen.

My heartfelt wish is that through these 7 Steps, you have begun to feel this connection more deeply, to trust in the wisdom that flows through you, and to embrace the love that has always been your birthright.

The *7 Steps to Reconnect with Your Guardian Angel* is more than a spiritual practice. It is the foundation for Ascension, a bridge between the seen and unseen, a pathway to awakening. It is an invitation to remember how to step into your highest self and live with clarity, love, and divine purpose:

**Step 1**: *Preparing a sacred space for angelic healing – Creating an environment of peace and high vibration.*

**Step 2:** *Creating a sacred altar – Anchoring your connection with the angelic realm.*

**Step 3:** *Grounding and balancing your energy centres – Strengthening your energetic foundation.*

**Step 4:** *Reconnecting with your Guardian Angel – Opening the channel for divine communication.*

**Step 5:** *Awakening the divine potential within – Embracing your higher intelligence and limitless capabilities.*

**Step 6:** *Closing your sacred space and grounding excess energy – Sealing your spiritual work with balance.*

**Step 7:** *Gratitude – Cultivating an open heart to receive divine blessings.*

These steps are not simply about personal transformation, they are part of a greater awakening. We are living in extraordinary times, where humanity is being called to rise, to remember and to co-create a world rooted in authentic love and truth.

The wisdom of the ancients, the sacred knowledge of Atlantis, and the divine intelligence that has guided souls for millennia are all coming forward now, at the perfect moment for our evolution.

I share these teachings with deep love and a genuine desire to support you on this path. Everyone can develop their higher intelligence, deepen their intuition, and step into their divine potential. This is not reserved for a select few, it is a gift available to all.

As you continue forward, know that you are guided, supported and deeply loved. Over time, you may find that asking for divine guidance becomes as natural as breathing. What once felt like a practice becomes a way of being quiet, steady presence in your life, gently leading you toward greater peace, wisdom, and joy.

Love, light and blessings,

*Marguerite*

# A Final Invitation

Before you close this book, I ask you to take a quiet moment to reflect on the journey you have begun. You have already taken the first steps and that is something uniquely beautiful. However, this is not the end it is only the beginning.

Let this book become a companion, a trusted friend, something you keep nearby a source of comfort and wisdom you can turn to whenever you need guidance or reassurance. Dip into its pages when you seek clarity, strength, or a gentle reminder that you are never alone. Your Guardian Angel is always by your side, waiting for you to reach out.

I invite you to nurture this connection, to trust in your divine guidance and to walk forward with an open heart. If you ever feel lost or uncertain, return to these pages. They will always be here to support you, to uplift you and to remind you of the light within.

And most importantly share your light. The world needs your kindness, your wisdom, your love. Let your journey inspire others and together, we will create a world where love, truth and divinity shine brightly for all.

You are exactly where you need to be. Everything you seek is already unfolding in perfect time.

Love light blessings.

*Marguerite.*

Printed in Dunstable, United Kingdom

68375166R00127